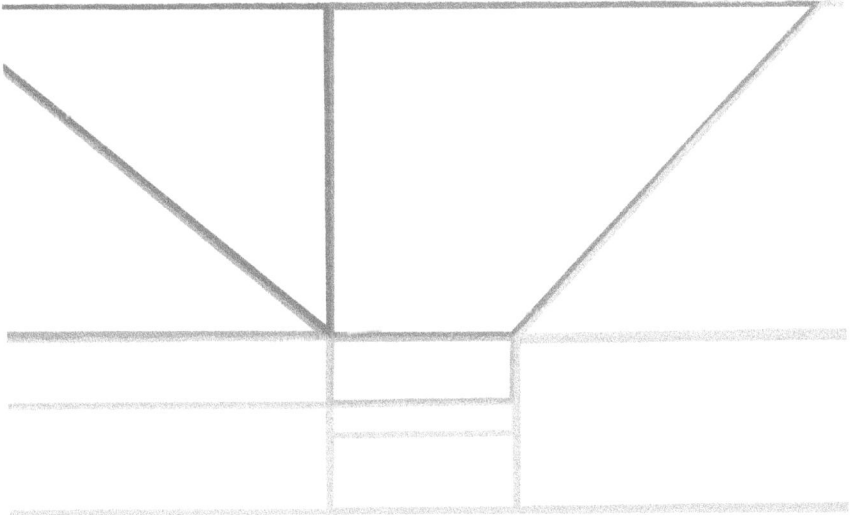
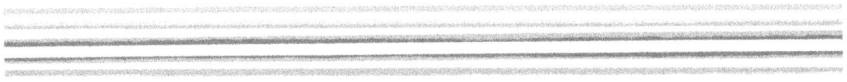

I DON'T
BELIEVE
IN POETRY

Legna Rodríguez Iglesias

Translated from the Spanish by Robin Myers
FOREWORD BY REINA MARÍA RODRÍGUEZ

ᴀ
'*Alliter*atïon

I DON'T BELIEVE IN POETRY| LEGNA RODRÍGUEZ IGLESIAS
Translated from the Spanish by Robin Myers
First edition in English in April 2024

© Legna Rodríguez Iglesias
© Foreword by Reina María Rodríguez
© Allieratïon Publishing, 2024

www.thealliteration.us

Design by Elena Roosen
Cover by Andrea Martínez
Proofreading by Tess Rankin & Félix García
Editorial Coordination by Amayra Velón

ISBN: 979-8-9896241-8-8

LEGNA'S HUNGERS

What you are is hungry. Voraciously hungry for a moral.
"Absalom, Omicron!"[1]

LRI

To write this prologue, I stripped myself of any prejudice I might have about what poetry is or isn't. And although this bilingual anthology of poems by Legna Rodríguez Iglesias opens with a declaration that grants the book its title ("I don't believe in poet ry"), I find myself moving from one book to another—*Gum, Fertile Truce, Thread+Thread, Give Me a Puff, Miami Century Fox* (sonnets), *My Bald Girlfriend and I Are Going to Have a Baby*, and previously unpublished texts—at a dizzying pace that draws me into a poetics reaffirmed by its own unerring negativity.

This poetics hauls rotten, discarded things out of the muck: "These things, and others, in content / show life swinging on rotten axis," writes Bukowski. Legna's axis also swings against the grain of anything that seems to promise hope, asserting it-self in marginal language without prudishness or lyricism. With cynicism, we might say: protection from any pain. It does so, moreover, with the suspicion of someone deft at transforming

---

1   Text published in the column 53 noviecitas by Legna Rodríguez Iglesias in *Hypermedia Magazine* (December 29, 2021).

banality into useful tools: "spit out your gum / I tell myself / throw out your gum."

And on the gum's journey through all the objects it approaches and contaminates (like the nuts and bolts that the Stalker tosses around the Zone) across Camagüey, Havana, and Miami, another place appears: the place of waste. There, to paraphrase the title of one poem, "the country you live in is never a country," framed like a map between tattooed gashes on dead tissue, seeking to restore, against loss ("Next digit. Now next rock. Now next tattoo") a poetics of negation "from my fingernails."

From the very beginning, in the poems excerpted from *Chicle*, Legna doesn't try to trick anyone with subterfuge: "who ever said I was interested in anything at all." Or "with the emotional ties that were my lot / I tied my shoes, never to return." In order to refuse to become what's expected, what others want her to be. In order to return not just to a place, but to a determination: that of an unruly little girl who defies a gesture as common as tying her shoelaces; a clear route along a risky, zigzagging path.

I could say that *I Don't Believe in Poetry*, following the chronological progression of the poems, constricts all time to the present. It forms a clearing around it. The here and now is presented as an attitude that confronts the past—even the past of treasured memories. There, this "I," which unquestionably once engaged and even wanted to believe in something, is dragged along by the same destructive, retrospective force that causes collisions and propels everything that was, or tried to be, in order to reaffirm itself as a contemporary "I," still lyrical in spite of itself.

"I would prefer not to"—that phrase from Melville's story "Bartleby, the Scrivener"—materializes mostly as ballast in Legna's here and now, where it narrates family legacy through a collection of deft, uninhibited, inconsequential gestures: "Any man in spectacles / is my dad / and any woman in spectacles / is my dad." She also uses it to abruptly truncate any social legacy in the form of all the shoulds that once overwhelmed her: "Which makes me wonder if I've ever / felt good in my country or abroad, / or if I need to leave to feel it."

In this sense, the only dead weight that can resist the onslaught of interrogations without any chance at real solutions, at least collectively, will turn out to be putting one's faith in poems during the creation and development of another more complex and singular innocence. Might this be a timely head-swap between the supposedly good girl she used to be and the one she no longer is? And will anyone actually be able to execute this somersault, I wonder? All I know is that Cuban literature has already suffered from so many good girls that it could use a kick in the other direction.

As for Legna's kick, neon lights shine over the established warnings, creating new ones. Because her poems are signposts more than anything else: stop signs to keep the others from crossing the useless line that mutilates every possible opening. She writes: "Jumping . . . on my gallbladder, on my / lungs, on my kidneys, on my liver, on my / muscles, on my ovary"—like in a childhood game of hopscotch, drawing with colorful chalk on the sidewalk. There, we find what's left of some impermanence, a broken, fragmented, minimalist game, through an "I" who remains unmoved by the turbulence of her time.

"There was a poverty around me," she writes in *Give Me a Puff*. As if these unlamented survivals were exposed only for the benefit of artistic creation, against a programmed fate that seeks to destroy the "I" (and especially its individual freedom), with a kick as well: "What I do with poetry is cover up the shit. / I cover and cover it. With my hands. With my feet."

And so the dichotomy of this boxing match between a marginal language and an "I" is resolved through the emergence of the "bad girl" character, who swings in dirty boots among the perversions and detritus yielded by said survival. She ties the laces of her sturdy shoes as if with flowers or butterflies: "My very first shoes were orthopedic."

Those narrow, rigid shoes repeatedly failed to correct this impulse, as well as the provocation against so-called formal education that power has always relished boasting about. In this way, the supposed "deviations" and "faults" shifted from the subject of aggression to the aggressor, like a boomerang whose means of seeing and feeling overcome the contradiction about what poetry is or isn't. The confrontation no longer exists between two types of language (one conversational and another more symbolic, as was once the case), nor is it Legna's concern.

After all, Legna doesn't resort to subterfuge, but positions herself between two ethical categories that will gradually become aesthetic ones—and the grounds for new tastes and appetites: "like yesterday's gum / another poem arising . . . / artificially flavored," she tells us. Or "And it was banana poison." Or "I believe in love. And tourism." Or "McDonald's vs. Pollo Tropical": "some go to McDonald's / some go / to Pollo Tropical." As if the dichotomy of any preference for food, color, flavor, gender, or place increasingly overcame her impatience.

This impatience will become a distinction that draws other commercial and media possibilities into her poetry—not only through products acquired on the market, everyday objects, their estrangements, their conflicts; not only through interaction with digital communication media, but through affection. It's an affection that loses romanticism and gains diversity: "That Slows after Flowering and Intensifies during the Milky Phase," as one title says. Or, in "Lips": "but when a woman / sucks another woman's tits / it means she loses everything / and gets it back / and loses everything / and gets it back." In this way, Legna loses everything and gets it back throughout these poems, again and again.

To begin what she herself calls "the milky phase," where she doesn't establish any comparisons or simulate any pleasure, or metaphors between alternative lexicons if they complement each other, or don't. Instead, she will become even more radicalized through the lack of identity that characterizes this "I."

Personally, I don't think there's anything more lyrical than this emptying out of identity: "I tugged on it that night / I tugged it with my mouth / and it was the first time I ever regretted anything."

She will even use metrical forms, sonnets, as protective jetties for the ships weighing anchor in a different bay from the one that first received her: "What happens if I founder in the mist?" There, she finds subsumed in that mist—stripped of the mystique of utopia and branded by consumption—the ghost of the helplessness that accompanied her. This is a lyrical helplessness, and it entails a still-greater one in striving to prove that the lyric—concealed in a discourse of money and abundance in such a different context—persists in rejecting everything that crosses its path and won't abandon it either here or there. "[A]nd you won't say / a peep," Legna writes, leaving us open-mouthed, bewildered.

She is doubly overwhelmed, then: by the fog enveloping a past of repression and slogans, confronted with new presages like will-o'-the-wisp, by the spattering of a screen in the small-town movie theater I mentioned. Because, starting with *Fertile Truce*, with a grandfather's death—"a pacemaker watching me," she writes—we find a break with family, legacy, and the codes it left her. What becomes more evident, if such a thing is even possible, is the demystification of her poetics in every context, especially the political one.

In "Cine Guerrero," for instance, Legna turns a courageous cultural act—fostered by the revolutionary epic through the name of a provincial movie theater—into a sexual one: "we spattered the screen." The poems joke and jeer, here and there, using irony to spatter, too, the double interpretation of the theater's name, as well as the screen transformed into the propagandistic billboard of a terrible era: discontinuous gestures, stains, allegorical names.

In "Special Period," "Made in Cuba," and "New Man," the chewing gum becomes a hot strip of adhesive tape, a makeshift remedy to shoddily cover a wound, "discarded on the side-walk." Here, too, the rudest forms of expression are superimposed over the political correctness of an ideological climate: "but you don't feel shit." A bad word becomes a shout, corroding her in the face of what she can no longer feel.

Both along the journey "from the word to Miami to work in Miami to Miami / to make money," where movement has, in these poems, a motive that is more economic than anything else, and in "Give Me a Puff" ("the puff's the very best part of all"; "take for instance / the president of the United States of America and see what it tastes like"), Legna seeks out flavors, smells, and gestures to demystify anything supposedly sacred.

And she finds it in any assessment that discredits the hierarchies of powers we might have granted the event, no matter what it may be, ranking it lower and lower: "I turned eighteen years old not long ago. / I oiled up my armpits and my pussy." Or, much later, when she mentions the book by Louise Glück she carries around in her backpack—inadequate documentation in the eyes of a police officer.

In the book *My Bald Girlfriend and I Are Going to Have a Baby*, the texts undergo a greater landslide between power and the personal: "How to explain / That you have two mothers / Instead of one." The tenderness foraged from the mother's body in "The Feeling of Peeing on a Pregnancy Test": "There's a faint line. / As faint as the fear of peeing / Again." A test to end the hungers accumulated and once again become the person, through her expanding belly (even when it doesn't show), who clarifies, in this contradiction between apparent wanting and not wanting, that the visible can offer another kind of refuge. She doesn't forget the color of her hunger: "white from the childhood of nineteen ninety-two I'm hungry Mamá."

As much as I'd like to issue a prophecy about the path that Legna's texts will follow, I can't. They carry on by trolley down the streets of Miami: "Ms. Trolley Remembers Countries," she writes in *Miami Century Fox*, gazing indifferently through the window. Then she'll leap through the broken pane, seeking the escaping present, the occasion.

When I read Legna's poem dedicated to Lorenzo García Vega, I suspected that her impulse was the key: "The Old Man Breathes Like I Move My Leg." The key to these intermittent movements, both visible and invisible, in shattering what was trapped inside a rhetoric that kept us from feeling something: "you can only get out of it by eliminating the drawing the child and you." You can get out of it only by doing away with nostalgia.

RMR
Miami, September 15, 2022

I DON'T
BELIEVE
IN POETRY

DE CHICLE
(AHORA ES CUANDO)[2]

FROM *GUM*
(THE TIME IS NOW)

[2] Limón Partido Collection, Mexico City: Proyecto Literal, 2013; Havana: Letras Cubanas, 2016.

Cálmate
me digo
concéntrate
me digo
toma las riendas de tu vida
azuza a los perros
ordénales que corran
bien lejos de aquí
corre
me digo
bien lejos de aquí
me digo
sigue las señales de los perros
más allá del final
pero tú no querrás escribir
un solo poema en tu vida
tú querrás escribir mil poemas
por lo menos
escupe el chicle
me digo
tira el chicle
me digo
o masticas o tomas las riendas
es tu negocio.

Calm down
I tell myself
pay attention
I tell myself
take the reins of your life
unleash the dogs
command them to run
far away from here
run
I tell myself
far away from here
I tell myself
follow the signals of the dogs
beyond the end
but you won't want to write
a single poem ever again
you'll want to write a thousand poems
at least
spit out your gum
I tell myself
throw out your gum
I tell myself
either spit or take the reins
that's your job.

Los collares que me pongo cuando voy al centro de la ciudad
a escribir sobre sus parques, sus árboles, sus transeúntes, y sus
    basuras
me los meto en la vesícula si estoy en casa
bien metidos allí, apretados, el vientre empieza a brincarme.
Dar brincos es lo que doy sobre los poemas que hice cuando fui
    al centro de la ciudad
quién dijo que me interesaban los parques, los árboles, los
    transeúntes, y las basuras
quién dijo que algo me interesaba.
Dar brincos es lo que di sobre los collares que me puse cuando
    fui al centro de la ciudad
quién dijo que con tales collares puestos
lograría escribir algo que sirviera
quién dijo que los collares me interesaban.
Dar brincos es lo que doy sobre mi propia vesícula,
    sobre mis pulmones, sobre mis riñones, sobre mi hígado, sobre mis
    músculos, sobre mi ovario
quién dijo que dar brincos sobre esa retahíla de órganos
era saludable
quién lo dijo, please.

The necklaces I wear when I go downtown
to write about the city's parks, its trees, its passersby, its trash—
I stick them in my gallbladder if I'm at home
all stuck in there, squeezed tight, my belly starts to jump.
Jumping is what I do on the poems I wrote the time I went
      downtown
whoever said I was interested in parks, in trees, in passersby, in
      trash
whoever said I was interested in anything at all.
Jumping is what I did on the necklaces I wore when I went
      downtown
whoever said that while wearing such necklaces
I'd manage to write anything worthwhile
whoever said I was interested in necklaces at all.
Jumping is what I do on my gallbladder,
      on my lungs, on my kidneys, on my liver, on my muscles,
      on my ovary
whoever said it was a healthy thing to jump on this whole
string of organs
whoever said it, *please.*

Nunca me gustó la frase lazos afectivos
por eso a través de mí nunca se posibilitaron este tipo de lazos
al conocer a alguien
y brindarle mi ayuda
para lo que necesites
mi casa está abierta para ti
involuntariamente pensaba
que más tarde o más temprano
me convertiría en una máquina de afecto
sabiendo que debía conservar cada uno de mis principios humanos
alteré el orden
cegué mis ojos,
no volví a ver a mi alrededor
con los lazos afectivos que me correspondían
amarré mis zapatos para no volver.

I never liked the phrase emotional ties
that's why such ties were never enabled by me
in meeting someone
and offering my help
whatever you need
my house is your house
I used to think involuntarily
that sooner or later
I'd turn into an affection machine
knowing I had to preserve every single one of my human
        principles
I altered the order
blinded my eyes,
never looked again at my surroundings
with the emotional ties that were my lot
I tied my shoes, never to return.

Ahora que me lo dices
recuerdo que desde ayer estoy aquí sentada
en este taburete
con los cinco dedos izquierdos metidos dentro del short
acariciándome los cañones
con los cinco dedos derechos apretando mi bolígrafo
lleno de tinta
mirando insistentemente la agenda
sobre el escritorio
sin escribir ni una sola palabra
cero palabra
cero pensamiento
un escritor me dijo que mi poesía era
una fórmula
algo parecido a dos más dos
o a tres más tres
pero yo tengo la seguridad
de que en todo caso
es algo parecido a ciento trece más doscientos doce
o a doscientos doce menos mil novecientos ochenta y cuatro
que es un año muy famoso
porque así se llama una novela
que no he leído
ahora que me lo dices
recuerdo que esa novela
nunca la he leído.

Now that you mention it
I realize I've been perched since yesterday
on this stool
with all five fingers of my left hand tucked into my shorts
caressing my stubble
and all five fingers of my right hand clutching my pen
charged with ink
staring intently at the agenda book
on my desk
not writing a word
zero words
zero thoughts
a male writer once told me that my poetry was
a formula
something along the lines of two plus two
or three plus three
but I have every confidence
that if anything
it's more like one hundred thirteen plus two hundred twelve
or two hundred twelve minus one thousand nine hundred
        eighty-four
which is a very famous year
because that's the title of a novel
I haven't read
now that you mention it
I realize I've never read
that novel.

Antes de este libro
escribí un libro que contenía
muchos poemas
en él todo giró
alrededor del 8
la realidad simbolizada
una situación desesperante
un objeto
de metal
salí risueña
de metal
los poemas de este libro
son muchos
también
y no me lo creo
no tiene gracia
de ningún modo.

Before this book
I wrote a book that had
lots of poems in it
the whole thing revolved
around the number 8
a symbol of reality
a desperate situation
a metal
object
I turned out cheerful
metal
this book
has lots of poems in it
as well
and I don't buy it
it has no point
at all.

Casi al despertar
doblada en los asientos de una Terminal de ómnibus
cuando los clientes que poseen reservación
para el turno de las seis y treinta
abordan su constante medio de transporte
el flujo de poesía es inminente
en mi bolsillo
un viejo chicle de ayer
desde mis uñas
otro poema que nace
saborizado
menta
fresa
melocotón
incorporando mi cuerpo al andén
reprimo el flujo.

Almost awake
folded across the seats in a bus station
when ticketed customers
for the six-thirty departure
board their steadfast means of transportation
the flow of poetry is imminent
in my pocket
like yesterday's gum
another poem arising
from my fingernails
artificially flavored
spearmint
strawberry
peach
incorporating my body onto the platform
I stifle the flow.

La impresora que imprimía de noche
está detrás de esa puerta
y esa puerta
está cerrada con llave
y la llave
está en tu estómago
dando saltos
de alegría
para que yo no imprima mi libro
tres copias solamente
a ver si gano un concurso
de varios miles de dólares
a ver si me compro
un creyón.

The printer that printed by night
is behind that door
and that door
is locked
and the key
is in your stomach
jumping
for joy
so that I won't print my book
just three copies
maybe I'll win a contest
worth several thousand dollars
maybe I'll buy myself
a crayon.

Esos pies los conozco de algún lado
y esa nariz
y ese escroto
sobre todo
lo conozco de algún lado
tú eres el que escribió ese poema que termina así:
«tu vagina o tu sandía
cualquiera de las dos
me las desayunaré»
asonancias
pero me gustas
me inquietas
si fueras una niña me inquietarías más
una niña con cola de caballo
dientes de caballo
almendra
tú eres el que escribió aquel poema
que ya yo había escrito mucho antes
hacía 24 horas
pero igual
fue un buen trabajo
para ti.

I know those feet from somewhere
and that nose
and that scrotum
most of all
I know it from somewhere
you're the guy who wrote the poem that ends like this:
your vagina or your watermelon
whatever
I'll eat them for breakfast
assonances
but I'm drawn to you
you unsettle me
if you were a girl you'd unsettle me more
a girl with a ponytail
horse teeth
almond
you're the guy who wrote that poem
I'd written long before
24 hours ago
but whatever
it was a good job
for you.

DE TREGUA FECUNDA[3]

FROM *FERTILE TRUCE*

---

3   Colección Manjuarí (Havana: Ediciones Unión 2012).

Tregua Fecunda

Sobre el ataúd de mi grandfather
hay flores nacionales
ese hombre luchó en una guerra
hace más de sesenta años
una guerra por la libertad
liberarse de lo que lo ata
es la lucha común.
Sabía leer y escribir
con cierta facilidad
pero no mejor que yo
fue una lástima
que quien practica la autopsia
le dejara el marcapasos
en el fondo de su pecho
ahora bajo las flores
hay un marcapasos vigilándome
¿Qué esperaba mi grandfather de mí?
¿Qué sembrara una flor nacional
en el fondo de mi corazón mangrino?
Que en paz descanses grandfather
ya escribí cosas grandfather
y esa es la mejor revolución
que haré.

Fertile Truce

My grandfather's coffin
is wreathed with national flowers
that man fought in a war
over sixty years ago
a war for liberty
liberation from what ties you down
is a common struggle.
He had a certain knack
for reading and writing
but no more than I do
it was a shame
that the coroner
left his pacemaker
in the depth of his chest
under the flowers
there's now a pacemaker watching me
What did my grandfather expect of me?
What could a national flower sow
in the depths of my meager heart?
Rest in peace gramps
I've written a thing or two gramps
and that's the best revolution
I'll ever wage.

Cine Guerrero

Asistir al cine constituyó, más que nuestra primera actividad cultural,
nuestra primera actividad sexual.
Observamos las películas desde cada una de sus butacas
y aprendimos que lo único malo de empezar a verlas
era terminar de verlas.
Una vez salpicamos la pantalla.
Lo sé porque la salpicadura continúa estando donde mismo.
De todas aquellas películas, recordamos algunas más que otras.
Pero de todas aquellas butacas, recordamos todas aquellas butacas.
De todos aquellos jóvenes que asistíamos al cine, sus butacas
solo nos recuerdan a nosotros.
Pero de todos aquellos jóvenes que empezaban a ver las
películas y no terminaban de verlas
nadie se acuerda.

Cine Guerrero

Going to the movies was less our first cultural activity
than our first sexual activity.
We watched the movies from every single seat
and learned that the only problem with starting to watch
was watching all the way to the end.
Once we spattered the screen.
I know because the spatter is still there.
Of all those movies, we remember some better than others.
But of all those seats, we remember all of those seats.
Of all the teenagers we were who went to the movies, their seats
      only remind us of us.
But of all those teenagers who started watching the movies and
      didn't watch all the way to the end,
no one remembers any of them.

Período especial

La gota de menstruación que resbala por mi sien
se parece a las gotas incansables de lluvia
o a las lágrimas del tocororo
la gota de menstruación rueda por mi nariz
moja mis labios
y vuelve
igual que yo me coloco
en el centro de una idea esta es la idea:
menstruar para siempre
por la mirilla veo tilapias
tencas
mi nariz atisba el sino
tararea la canción
contiene al silencio
transfigura
igual que las tilapias
transfigura.

Special Period

The drop of menstrual blood that trickles down my temple
is like the tireless drops of rain
or the tears of the tocoroco bird
the drop of menstrual blood slips down my nose
moistens my lips
and returns
just as I place myself
in the center of an idea this is the idea:
to menstruate forever
I see tilapia through the peephole
tenches
my nose catches the fate
hums the song
contains the silence
transfigures
just like tilapia
it transfigures.

Vivir es morir

El camino que conduce
al seno donde nací
está lleno de leopardos
(yo tengo más que el leopardo
porque tengo mucho sueño)
después de que los leopardos
eyaculan sobre el césped
se vuelven medio neuróticos
yo estoy medio neurótica
medio hambrienta
temo que me pondré
como una leoparda ruina
lo temo todo excepto el ocio
en el ocio me quedaría
hasta la muerte.

To Live Is to Die

The road that leads
to the breast where I was born
is chock-full of leopards
(I have more than the leopard
because I'm sleepy)
once the leopards
ejaculate onto the lawn
they get kind of neurotic
kind of hungry
I fear I'll end up
like a wild she-leopard
I fear everything except leisure
I'd gladly linger in leisure
till I die.

Hombre Nuevo

Grandfather tiene el mundo cubierto de esplendores
conforme al hombre nuevo
grandfather tiene el mundo cubierto de conformidades
en las márgenes de su río
crecen cabezas de ajo
¿qué hiciste grandfather
cuando fuiste a la mar por primera vez?
¿jugaste con la arena y con los cubos de arena?
Grandfather me acaricia
y le salen unas alas muy hermosas
esas alas tan hermosas
deberían salirme a mí.

New Man

Grandfather has the world covered in splendor
in accordance with the new man
Grandfather has the world covered in accordances
on the edges of his river
heads of garlic grow
What did you do, Grandfather,
when you saw the ocean for the first time?
Did you play with the sand and with buckets of sand?
Grandfather caresses me
and sprouts beautiful wings
those beautiful wings
should be mine.

Cría Fama

Había un esparadrapo caliente
reforzando el algodón
en la llaga caliente de San Lazarus
también había virtud
en ese gesto constante de reforzar
San Lazarus se daba cuenta
y lloraba.
Había un esparadrapo caliente
tirado en la acera
pero a mi llaga caliente
con su algodón guindando
nadie la reforzaba
mirando el esparadrapo
desde la acera del frente
yo me daba cuenta
y lo recogía.

Laurels

There was a strip of hot adhesive tape
reinforcing the cotton ball
on the hot stigmata of Saint Lazarus
there was also virtue
in that unerring gesture of reinforcement
Saint Lazarus noticed it
and wept.
There was a strip of hot adhesive tape
discarded on the sidewalk
but no one reinforced
my own hot stigmata
with its dangling cotton ball
staring at the adhesive tape
from across the street
I noticed
and retrieved it.

Hecho en Cuba

Enfisema pulmonar para surcar el aire
con un tenedor de acero
y un reloj Casio que marca
las 12:17 minutos
¿de la noche? ¿del día?
pero yo te icé primero
para que tú me izaras después
¿qué te importa que te ice?
para surcar el cielo
con un reloj Casio que marca
las 12:18 minutos
¿de la noche? ¿del día?
y enfisema pulmonar
en cada músculo de mis piernas
por eso dejé de correr detrás de mí
con un tenedor de acero
para clavarme el tenedor
en el enfisema
y detenernos
el enfisema y yo
a las 12:19 minutos
¿de la noche? ¿del día?

Made in Cuba

Pulmonary emphysema to plow the air
with a steel fork
and a Casio watch that marks
12:17
p.m.? a.m.?
But I lifted you first
so you'd lift me later
what do you care if I lift you?
to plow the sky
with a Casio watch that marks
12:18
p.m.? a.m.?
and pulmonary emphysema
in every muscle of my legs
that's why I stopped running after myself
with a steel fork
to stab the fork
into my emphysema
and stop us
the emphysema and me
at 12:19
p.m.? a.m.?

Cereza Podrida

Uno cree que al bajar
La Avenida de Los Presidentes
va a sentir alivio
seguridad
tal vez admiración
o por el contrario náusea
pero uno no siente ni pinga
el océano a lo lejos es lo más pesado que hay
un cielo en la tierra
un valle de agua por gusto
atravieso la Avenida
sintiendo todo lo que puedo sentir
y un niño me grita loca porque hablo sola
me hablaba a mí misma del amor
de los deseos que tengo de que chupen mi cereza
pero yo no estoy para menores
yo podría despingar a su madre con mi puño
y luego echarla al océano
con todos los presidentes
mirándome.

Rotten Cherry

You think as you walk down
Avenida de los Presidentes
that you'll feel relief
confidence
even admiration
or alternatively nausea
but you don't feel shit
there's nothing heavier than the ocean in the distance
a sky on earth
a valley of water just for fun
I cut across the Avenida
feeling everything I can
and a kid calls me crazy for talking to myself
I was telling myself about love
and how much I want someone to suck my cherry
but I'm not into minors
I could beat the shit out of his mother
then toss her into the ocean
with all those presidents
watching me.

DE HILO+HILO[4]

FROM *THREAD+THREAD*

---

4   Leiden: Bokeh Press, 2015.

El Hilo

Yo jamás había visto un hilo en una vagina
colgando de la vagina como un moco de catarro
como un pañuelo de fiebre
> *yo jamás había halado un hilo de una vagina*
> *se le iba a salir el alma*
> *se le iba a ir con el hilo la memoria del horror*
yo lo halé aquella noche
> *lo halé con la boca*
> *y fue la primera vez que me arrepentí de algo.*

The Thread

I'd never seen a thread in a vagina before
hanging from the vagina like a line of snot
like a damp cloth for a fever
      I'd never tugged on a thread from a vagina
      the soul was going to tumble out of it
      the memory of horror was going to tumble right out with
      the thread
I tugged on it that night
      I tugged it with my mouth
      and it was the first time I ever regretted anything.

Como yo muevo la pierna el hombre viejo respira

Cuando escribí este poema en noviembre de 2011,
Lorenzo García Vega todavía estaba vivo.
El día de su muerte, viernes 1 de junio de 2012,
Reina María nos comentaba que lo había ido
a ver al hospital y que todo iba a estar bien
porque él tenía ganas de vivir.

La foto de Motorola no es lo mismo que la foto de BlackBerry
el poema de Lorenzo García Vega no es lo mismo que la foto de
Motorola
y tampoco es lo mismo que la foto de BlackBerry
la ropa interior Suchel Lever no es lo mismo que la ropa interior Calvin
Klein
el poema de Lorenzo García Vega es un poema interior
en menos de lo que Lorenzo García Vega termina de escribir
la ropa interior Suchel Lever deja ver un trozo de nalga
con el dedo en Motorola le tiro foto a la nalga y movida
con otro dedo en BlackBerry le tiro foto a la nalga y Calvin Klein.

The Old Man Breathes Like I Move My Leg

When I wrote this poem in November 2011,
Lorenzo García Vega was still alive.
On the day of his death, Friday, June 1, 2012,
Reina María told us that she'd visited him
at the hospital and everything was going to be all right
because he wanted to live.

A Motorola photo isn't the same as a BlackBerry photo
a poem by Lorenzo García Vega isn't the same as a Motorola
    photo
and it isn't the same as a BlackBerry photo
Suchel Lever underwear isn't the same as Calvin Klein
    underwear
in less time than it takes for Lorenzo García Vega to finish
    writing
the Suchel Lever underwear exposes a section of ass
with a finger on Motorola I snap a photo of the ass, and blurrily
with another finger on BlackBerry I snap a photo of the ass and
    Calvin Klein.

Labios

Que a una mujer
le chupen las tetas
pezones, aureola y borde
significa que pierda el camino
y lo recupere
mientras le siguen chupando
pezones, aureola
pero que una mujer
le chupe las tetas a otra
significa que pierda todo
y lo recupere
y pierda todo
y lo recupere
y cuando lo recupere
se dé cuenta de que todo
no era nada
comparado con el resto.

Lips

When a woman gets
her tits sucked
nipples, areola and edge
it means she loses her way
and gets it back
as her nipples and areola
are further sucked
but when a woman
sucks another woman's tits
it means she loses everything
and gets it back
and loses everything
and gets it back
and when she gets it back
she realizes that everything
was nothing
compared to all the rest.

El orden de los factores

Se supone que si esta
se ubica sobre aquella
lo que ocurre es la tortilla
yo me ubico sobre ti
y lo que ocurre es la tortilla
además me ubico abajo
y lo que ocurre es la tortilla
además me muevo un poco
y lo que ocurre es la tortilla
además lo que ocurre
es muy sabroso
la tortilla son dos partes
las dos partes son iguales
la tortilla hay que ensayarla
una tortilla legítima
no se rompe fácilmente
hacer tortilla
no es fácil.

Order of Operations

If this is placed
on top of that
the result is a tortilla
If place myself on top of you
the result is a tortilla
and if I place myself under you
the result is a tortilla
and if I move a little
the result is a tortilla
in any case what happens
is delicious
a tortilla has two parts
the two parts are equal
making a tortilla takes practice
an authentic tortilla
isn't easily broken
making a tortilla
isn't easy.

Leer y escribir

Una cosa inolvidable
fue el chocolate espeso caliente
con pimienta y nuez moscada
otra cosa inolvidable
fue el pezón que puso en mi vagina
porque cuando lo puso
escribió con el pezón
quiero escribir un poema
y el chocolate espeso caliente
con pimienta y nuez moscada
comenzó a derramárseme
por el bollo
y todo la nuez moscada
se hizo lenguaje
en mi boca
y al derramárseme lo que nunca
se me había derramado
salió entonces un yogurt
de monilias asesinas
y matar las monilias
me gustó
cantidad.

Reading and Writing

One unforgettable thing
was the thick hot chocolate
with pepper and nutmeg
another unforgettable thing
was the nipple placed in my vagina
because once it was there
it wrote with the nipple
I want to write a poem
and the thick hot chocolate
with pepper and nutmeg
started spilling right out
of my pussy
and all the nutmeg
turned to language
in my mouth
and in spilling what had never
spilled out of me
what emerged was yogurt
with killer fungus
and when I killed the fungus
I liked it
very much.

Tiene relieve

Ten cuidado
si te encuentras
con un novio hembra
por la calle
porque es un fenómeno
del que no te salvarás
ni en tablitas
morderá tus hombros
morderá tus labios
y ni el médico chino
te salvará
hará círculos
con su lengua
primero en una aureola
y luego en la otra aureola
y tú no dirás
ni mú
a los cinco minutos
descubrirá tu tatuaje
expresará consternado
tiene relieve
pero ya no podrás
ponerle freno a nada
y no sabrás
por qué.

Raised

Be careful
if you run
into a female boyfriend
on the street
because it's a phenomenon
that won't spare you
not a chance
she'll bite your shoulders
she'll bite your lips
and not even Chinese medicine
will save you
she'll make circles
with her tongue
first around one areola
then the other areola
and you won't say
a pccp
within five minutes
she'll discover your tattoo
and say, dismayed,
it feels raised
but it'll be too late
for you to put the brakes on anything
and you won't
know why.

Mamá y papá

Cualquier hombre con espejuelos
es mi papá
y cualquier mujer con espejuelos
es mi papá
por eso aprecio a los hombres
y me acerco a las mujeres
porque no hay nada como una persona
que sea mamá y papá
al mismo tiempo
y me duerma y me despierte
al mismo tiempo
y me bese y me sacuda
y me dé dulces
y me dé golpes
los espejuelos deben tener
la montura plástica.

Mom and Dad

Any man in spectacles
is my dad
and any woman in spectacles
is my dad
that's why I appreciate men
and approach women
because there's nothing like a person
who's both mom and dad
at the same time
and who lulls me to sleep and wakes me up
at the same time
and who kisses and shakes me
and gives me candy
and hits me
the spectacles must
have plastic frames.

El hilo

Una vez vi un hilo colgando de una vagina
y lo halé pensando que de adentro
las cosas no se desprenden por gusto
no me arrepentí por lo que hubiera podido desprenderse
sino porque se desprendió algo insignificante
algo que hubiera podido ser el alma
pero que no fue el alma de ninguna manera
apenas un moco mal anudado.

The Thread

Once I saw a thread hanging from a vagina
and I tugged it thinking that things
don't detach for no reason inside
I didn't regret what might have detached
I regretted that it was something insignificant
something that could have been the soul
but wasn't the soul in any sense
just a poorly knotted line of snot.

DE DAME SPRAY[5]

FROM *GIVE ME A PUFF*

5   Madrid: Hypermedia Ediciones, 2016.

Una Oración

De pronto, en medio de la noche, una oración.
Me tenía prohibido a mí misma comenzar cualquier cosa
con esa frase de pronto,
sin embargo ahí, en medio de la noche,
algo peor que de pronto,
estaba aquello, una oración.
En la cocina llené mi copa,
el agua tenía escarcha así que fue interesante sentir
esos cristales descendiendo por la lengua.
Era el calor, y estaba, como una absoluta apropiación
de todo el ser y el estar juntos
allí, en ese espacio y en ese tiempo, una oración.
Era el dolor, también, más de frente que de cabeza,
hacía casi una semana.
Y era el veneno de plátano, medicina natural compuesta
por alcohol y plátano.
Había una pobreza a mi alrededor que yo no podía
creer pero sí identificar.
Como tantas otras noches coloqué el doble candado,
bebí otra copa pensando en los cristales,
derretidos y tibios, a esa altura.
Fui apagando cada luz, cada bondad.
La oración se quedó para después.

A Prayer

All of a sudden, in the middle of the night, a prayer.
I'd forbidden myself from starting anything
with that phrase, *all of the sudden*,
and yet, *in the middle of the night*,
which is worse than *all of the sudden*,
there it was, a prayer.
I filled my glass in the kitchen.
The water was icy, so it was interesting to feel
the crystals slipping down my tongue.
It was the heat, and it was, like an absolute appropriation
of my entire being and of being together
there, in that space and in that time, a prayer.
It was also pain, more head-on than upside-down,
for over a week at that point.
And it was banana poison, a natural remedy made
from alcohol and bananas.
There was a poverty around me that I couldn't
believe but could identify.
As on so many other nights, I clicked the double padlock shot,
drank another glass, thinking about the crystals,
melted, lukewarm by then.
I switched off every light, every virtue.
I left the prayer for later.

Ante tu experiencia cultural y emocional,
¿Qué más puedo aportarle a tu vida?

Una circunferencia cefálica
provista de treinta y cinco centímetros.
Un cuello corto, sin tumoraciones palpables, ni pliegues.
La cabeza. El tronco. Las extremidades.
Miembros cortos en relación con el tronco.
En la planta de los pies, pliegues gruesos y profundos.
A lo largo de mi busto, pezón teñido, relieve y margen.
Botones mamarios. Ingurgitación. Plastilina. Tierra.
Apéndice xifoides en el esternón. Protrusión en el epigastrio.
La hernia umbilical es frecuente en nuestro medio,
y generalmente no requiere tratamiento.
Estertores húmedos finos denominados
estertores de desplegamiento.
Meconio. Líquido amniótico. Moco.
Fermentos digestivos. Bilis.
Epitelios descamados. Pelos deglutidos.
En cuestiones de segundos la placenta
como objeto perderá toda importancia,
y su huella, círculo ácido en el asiento,
será necesario quitarla.
La pérdida inicial de peso
puede ser explicada
en relación con el gasto calórico.
Luces y sombras.
El calostro que aporta la madre
rico en proteínas y anticuerpos
se queda por debajo del conflicto.
Individuo a término
porque ha nacido entre las treinta y siete
y las cuarenta y dos semanas.

Given Your Cultural and Emotional Experience, What Else Can I Contribute to Your Life?

A cephalic circumference
furnished with thirty-five centimeters.
Short neck, without folds or palpable tumorations.
Head. Torso. Extremities.
Limbs short in relation to the torso.
On the soles of the feet, thick, deep creases.
Around my bust, dyed nipple, relief and margin.
Mammary buttons. Ingurgitation. Play-Doh. Soil.
Xiphoid process in the sternum. Protrusion in the epigastrium.
The umbilical hernia is common in our circles
and generally doesn't require treatment.
Fine damp rattles called
deployment rattles.
Meconium. Amniotic fluid. Mucus.
Digestive fermentations. Bile.
Peeled epithelia. Deglutinated hairs.
In a matter of seconds, the placenta
will lose all importance as an object,
and the trace of it, acidic circle on the seat,
will have to be removed.
The initial weight loss
can be explained
in relation to caloric consumption.
Light and shadows.
The colostrum contributed by the mother,
rich in protein and antibodies,
remains beneath the conflict.
Individual to term,
because he was born between thirty-seven
and forty-two weeks.

Individuo a término
porque ha pesado entre dos mil quinientos gramos
y cuatro coma cinco kilogramos.
Individuo a término porque ha llorado.
Se está produciendo una toma de conciencia
en la que cada vez más
la masa x la velocidad es = a poder.

Entonces había sido capaz de crear un lenguaje plástico
a nivel de vacío, silencio, analfabetismo
lo suficientemente poderoso y propio
como para acurrucarme
bajo una selva de espinas y dormir.

Individual to term,
because he weighed between twenty-five hundred grams
and four point five kilograms.
Individual to term, because he cried.
Awareness is being raised
in which increasingly
mass x velocity = power.
So I'd been able to create a visual language
on the level of void, silence, illiteracy
powerful and personal enough
for me to curl up
in a jungle of thorns and sleep.

Un proceso acumulativo de materia seca
que después de la floración es lento
y se va intensificando durante la fase lechosa

El primer reloj de mi vida fue de juguete.
Las agujas se movían si yo movía la mano.
Los primeros zapatos de mi vida fueron ortopédicos.
Las agujas se movían si yo movía la mano.
El primer viaje de mi vida fue ilegal
La Habana-Lima y Lima-Santo Domingo
con una visa falsa bajo una tormenta llamada Ernesto.
El primer perfume de mi vida fue a los veintisiete años.
Jengibre francés, me parece.
Tengo un abuelo por parte de padre, llamado Ernesto.
Me parece.

A Cumulative Process of Dry Matter
That Slows after Flowering
and Intensifies during the Milky Phase

My very first watch was a toy.
The hands moved if I moved my hand.
My very first shoes were orthopedic.
The hands moved if I moved my hand.
My very first trip was illegal
Havana–Lima and Lima–Santo Domingo
with a fake visa during a storm called Ernesto.
My very first perfume was at age twenty-seven.
French ginger, I believe.
I have a paternal grandfather named Ernesto.
I believe.

Toma de conciencia

La apertura es asombrosa,
mi colonia celular va creciendo lentamente,
se mantiene encapsulada,
y sus unidades mantienen
una morfología y biología normales,
así que no contagia los tejidos aledaños
y mucho menos afecta otros órganos.
Después ya no se sabe,
fuga hacia otra forma más irregular,
invade
o destruye lo que rodea y en su progresión genera
desprendimientos de estructuras idénticas a sí,
capaces de trasladarse a otros tejidos y órganos,
por canales que no puedo recordar,
constituyendo depósitos, colonizándome,
un efecto conocido con el nombre de metástasis.

Los familiares lloran, gritan, discuten.
Cada media hora o menos
un desfile de personas que ni siquiera conozco
hace acto de presencia en nuestro hogar.
Conversan, comen, toman agua, van al baño,
invaden o destruyen lo que rodean
y en su progresión generan
desprendimientos de estructuras idénticas a sí,
capaces de trasladarse,
por canales que no puedo recordar,
constituyendo depósitos, colonizándome,
un efecto conocido con el nombre de metástasis.

Awareness-Raising

The opening is wondrous,
my cellular colony slowly expands,
remains encapsulated,
and its units maintain
normal morphology and biology,
so it doesn't infect the neighboring tissues,
much less affect other organs.
After that, who knows.
It escapes into a more erratic form,
invades
or destroys what's around it, causing, as it progresses,
the detachments of structures identical to itself,
capable of transfer onto other tissues and organs,
through channels I can't remember,
constituting deposits, colonizing me,
an effect known as metastasis.

My relatives weep, shout, fight.
Every half hour or less
a parade of people I don't even know
makes an appearance in our home.
They chat, eat, drink water, go to the bathroom,
invade or destroy what's around them,
causing, as they progress,
the detachments of structures identical to them,
capable of transfer
through channels I can't remember,
constituting deposits, colonizing me,
an effect known as metastasis.

El hermano de mi novia

El hermano de mi novia no parece una persona.
La forma de su cuerpo no es la de un ser humano.
Y eso me hace preguntarme
si la forma de mi cuerpo es la de un ser humano.
O por el contrario me parezco a mi cuñado,
un hombre sin pensamiento que necesita
irse de su país para poder sentir bienestar.
Está enamorado de una mujer como él sin pensamiento
que necesita irse de su país para poder sentir bienestar.
Y eso me hace preguntarme si alguna vez
he sentido bienestar dentro de mi país o fuera
o si necesito irme de él para poder sentirlo.
Es a lo que me refiero cuando digo
que el tipo no parece una persona
porque evidentemente tiene todo en su vida:
una mujer que lo ama.
Y eso me hace preguntarme si yo tengo todo en la vida.

My Girlfriend's Brother

My girlfriend's brother doesn't seem like a person.
His body isn't shaped like a human body.
And this makes me wonder
if my body is shaped like a human body.
Or if, alternatively, I look like my girlfriend's brother,
a man without thoughts, who needs
to leave his country to feel good.
He's in love with a woman without thoughts, like him,
who needs to leave her country to feel good.
Which makes me wonder if I've ever
felt good in my country or abroad,
or if I need to leave to feel it.
This is what I mean when I say
that the guy doesn't seem like a person
because clearly he has everything in life:
a woman who loves him.
Which makes me wonder if I have everything in life.

Billetes de a cinco y a veces de a diez

El último viejo cañengo camina con un bastón por una calle de tierra.
Le robo billetes de a cinco y a veces billetes de a diez.
Ganas no me faltan de robarle billetes de a veinte y a veces billetes de
    a cincuenta.
Incluso billetes de a cien.
Se los robo del bolsillo derecho del pantalón y a veces del bolsillo
    izquierdo.
Incluso de los bolsillos de atrás donde el viejo esconde sus retorcidos
    billetes.
La meningoencefalitis camina con un bastón por una calle de tierra.
La meningoencefalitis se llevó al viejo cañengo.
Fue lo último que se llevó.
Ganas no me faltan, de todo.

Five- and Sometimes Ten-Peso Bills

The last old geezer walks with a cane down a dirt road.
I steal five- and sometimes ten-peso bills from him.
I can't say I don't want to steal some twenty- and sometimes
    fifty-peso bills.
Even a hundred.
I pluck them from his right pants pocket and sometimes from
    the left.
Even from the back pockets where the old man hides his
    crumpled bills.
Meningoencephalitis walks with a cane down a dirt road.
Meningoencephalitis took the old geezer.
It was the last thing it took.
I can't say I don't want anything at all.

Teatro Alemán

Después de ver una puesta en escena
escrita y producida por su director
todo lo que necesito es un café americano humeante
que me caliente los dedos y la palma,
que me provoque una insigne lesión en el esófago
porque el pensamiento y las emociones
ya se chamuscaron desde el minuto catorce.

Y más necesito tu lengua.
Un lengüetazo en cada mejilla.

Teatro Alemán

After watching a play
written and produced by its director
all I need is a steaming Americano
to heat my fingers and palms,
to cause notable damage to my esophagus,
because my thoughts and emotions
were already charred at minute fourteen.

Even more than that, I need your tongue.
A lick on each cheek.

Masa x velocidad

Cuando le concedan la palabra oprima el botón verde
cuando se ilumine la indicación roja del micrófono
puede hacer uso de la palabra
evite tocar el micrófono mientras habla
manténgase a una distancia de veinte a treinta centímetros
del micrófono mientras habla
bajo el sufrimiento del ciclo menstrual
no haga uso de la palabra
y tampoco bajo el sufrimiento de la falta de aire
lo mejor de todo es el uso de la palabra
en caso de ser palabra en desuso use el spray
lo mejor de todo es el spray.

Mass x Velocity

When given the floor, press the green button
when the mic's red light turns on
the floor is yours
avoid touching the microphone as you speak
maintain a distance of twenty to thirty centimeters
from the microphone as you speak
if afflicted by your menstrual cycle
don't take the floor
the same applies if you're afflicted by a lack of air
the very best part is taking the floor
and if air feels thin up there, then take a puff
the puff's the very best part of all.

DE TÍTULO[6]

FROM *TITLE*

---

6   Chicago: Kenning Editions, 2020.

11

cotorra que ladra y muerde es solo un tipo de estrangulamiento
la ventana es otro tipo y tirarse por ella es solo un puñado de
    mierda al aire
los libros de papel y las guías telefónicas dejan mucho que
    pensar
el niño sobre la mesa dibujando un monstruo existe nada más
    en mi imaginación
la taza sanitaria con veinte centímetros de diarrea canta el
    manisero
si te quieres por el pico divertir besa a la cotorra que ladra y
    muerde
reventándole la frente al niño no mataría dos pájaros de un tiro
reventándole la cabeza a la cotorra no mataría dos pájaros de
    un tiro
tendrían que ser dos niños dibujando sobre la mesa dos
    monstruos
y cuarenta centímetros de diarrea cantando en la taza sanitaria
o tendrían que ser dos cotorras ladrándome y mordiéndome
a mí no me gustan las aves ni los pescados ni los reptiles
ni ningún animal que no exprese varios signos de emoción

11

a barking biting parrot is just one kind of strangulation
the window is another and throwing yourself out of it is just a
    fistful of shit in midair
paper tomes and telephone books are really food for thought
the kid on the table drawing a monster exists only in my
    imagination
the toilet bowl with twenty centimeters of diarrhea sings the
    manisero song
if your beak would like some fun then kiss the barking biking
    parrot
smashing in the kid's forehead wouldn't kill two birds with one
    stone
smashing in the parrot's head wouldn't kill two birds with one
    stone
it'd have to be two kids drawing on the table two monsters
and forty centimeters of diarrhea singing in the toilet bowl
or two parrots barking at me biting me
I don't like birds or fish or reptiles
or any other animal that doesn't speak with exclamation points

44

mi doctora privada que antes fue mi novia y antes fue mi amiga
    y antes mi enemiga
y me obligaba a meterme bajo duchas de agua fría para bajarme
    la fiebre
del dengue o la desesperanza del dengue y de la desesperanza
me recomienda dormir de siete a nueve horas diarias cada día o
    cada noche
el momento que yo elija para hacerlo me incumbe solo a mí y no
    es problema
la cantidad de horas aconsejadas resulta casi imposible de llevar
    a cabo
comer no ayuda leer no ayuda reír no ayuda llorar no ayuda
    correr no ayuda pelear no
el efecto más común con la falta total o parcial de sueño es sin
    duda melancólico
un efecto que supongo extraño para la mayoría de los hombres y
    las mujeres actuales
por implicar algo conocido con el nombre de emoción palabra
    tildada en la última sílaba
sin embargo muchos otros factores de salud a nivel físico y
    psíquico intervienen aquí
mi doctora privada me recomienda dormir ocho horas si es
    preciso junto a ella
la cantidad de horas aconsejadas resulta casi imposible de llevar
    a cabo
ni qué decir del cómo el cuándo y el dónde metodológicamente
    antiéticos
la cama se encuentra localizada junto a la pared de manera vertical
la mesa es lo único plano que veo parada en puntas de pie desde
    este ángulo
sin embargo muchos otros factores de salud intervienen en mi
    modo de ver las cosas

44

my doctor who used to be my girlfriend and my friend before
        that and my enemy before that
and who used to make me take cold showers to keep the fever
        down
from dengue and the despair of dengue and despair in general
recommends I get seven to nine hours of sleep each day or night
the decision of when to do so is mine alone and it's not a problem
the number of advisable hours proves nearly impossible to
        fulfill
eating doesn't help reading doesn't help crying doesn't help or
        running or fighting
the most common effect of the total or partial lack of sleep is
        melancholy no question
an effect that must be strange to most contemporary men and
        women
to suggest something familiar by the name of emotion, a word
        accented in Spanish on the final syllable
however many other aspects of both physical and psychological
        health are relevant here
my doctor recommends I get eight hours of sleep beside her if
        necessary
the number of advisable hours proves nearly impossible to
        fulfill
and don't get me started on the methodologically antithetical
        when and where
the bed stands vertically against the wall
the table is the only plane I can see standing on tiptoe at that
        angle
however many other aspects of health are relevant to my
        perspective

a la playa a bañarse en la playa a la mar a ahogarse y perderse
a ver el océano y saber qué es el océano en el sentido patético/
ético/estético
de la palabra a Miami a trabajar en Miami a Miami
a conseguir dinero
a Miami a gozar a Canaán a Jerusalén a Egipto
el presidente de Egipto vino a Cuba a bañarse en la playa y dejó
su bikini en la arena
el presidente de Miami es una mujer calva que tiene muy buenas
condiciones vocales pero no tiene bikini
la angustia del pueblo es la misma que la del presidente
ojalá que tus piernas se conviertan en dos piernas
de jamón ahumado y se te pongan duras y se te echen a perder
quiero comida de presidente y más que eso quiero bikini
quiero comida y bikini de presidente y más que eso quisiera avión

99

to the beach to swim at the beach in the sea to drown and lose
     yourself
to gaze out at the ocean and know it's the ocean in the pathetic
     ethical/aesthetic sense
from the word to Miami to work in Miami to Miami
to make money
to Miami to revel in Canaan Jerusalem Egypt
the president of Egypt came to Cuba to swim at the beach and
     left
his bikini in the sand
the president of Miami is a bald woman with excellent
vocal conditions but no bikini
the people's distress is the same as the president's
if only your legs could become two legs
of smoked ham and stiffen and spoil
I want president food and more than that I want bikini
I want food and president bikini and more than that I'd like
     airplane

33

también octubre es un mes cruel un mes del que huiré toda mi vida
tumbada en mi rincón los árboles que brotan junto a mí me hablan
y mis hombros horribles en forma de círculos abultados empiezan
a ponerse alérgicos
esto quiere decir llenos de un prurito rojo que agrede incluso a la
oscuridad
para colmo mi madre de sangre que es además mi madre poética
y mi madre
en todos los sentidos posibles de elucubrar cumple años este día
como cada año
y coincide en número con el día en que naciera un hombre
llamado Ezra Pound
la llamo por teléfono para decírselo y antes de decírselo le digo
tengo hambre mamá
hambre de algo delicioso no de este arroz blanco en chapapotes
blancos sobre un plato
blanco de la infancia de mil novecientos noventa y dos tengo
hambre mamá
de un poema de Ezra Pound léeme el poema que tú quieras por
teléfono
hambre de un poema que diga cosas malas de ver y que los
árboles tengan
que ver hambre de un poema del que empiece a huir toda mi vida

33

October is also a cruel month I'll be fleeing all my life
sprawled in my corner the trees sprouting close by all speak
    to me
and my horrible shoulders in the shape of lumpy circles
    startgetting allergic
which means filled with a red pruritus that aggravates even the
    darkness
as if that weren't enough it's the birthday of my blood mother
    who is also my poetic mother
and my mother in all possible senses of conception like it is every
    year
and it overlaps in number with the birthday of a man named
    Ezra Pound
I call her on the phone to say so and before I say so I tell her I'm
    hungry Mamá
hungry for something delicious not this gluey smear of white
    rice on a plate
white from the childhood of nineteen ninety-two I'm hungry
    Mamá
for a poem by Ezra Pound read me any poem you want over the
    phone
hungry for a poem that says unsightly things with trees
in it hungry for a poem I'll start to flee from my whole life

88

el niño sobre la mesa ha estado dibujando un paisaje con
    llanura y árbol
el típico dibujo donde aparecen el padre la madre y el hijo
    figuras representativas
dentro de un sistema por eso al principio creí que era un
    monstruo tal vez
asocié una idea con otra o tal vez me falló la vista en todo caso es
    un dibujo
desesperante por una parte e inverosímil por otra en todo caso
    el dibujo está ahí
listo para ser estrujado y echado a la basura junto con el niño y
    la mesa
una mesa tan ridícula como el dibujo y tan inconsistente como
    un niño
al ver la noticia en internet acerca de un homicidio que incluía a
    un niño
deduje que el niño se había puesto a dibujar este tipo de paisaje
    que saca
a cualquiera de quicio y que te conduce a un estado tal de imbecilidad
desde donde solo es posible salir eliminando al dibujo al niño y a ti

88

the child on the table has been drawing a landscape with a tree
    and a meadow
the typical drawing with a father mother and son representative
    figures
within a system that's why at first I thought it was a monster
    maybe
I associated one idea with another or maybe my vision failed in
    any case it's a drawing
it's exasperating in one sense and unrealistic in another but in
    any case the drawing's there
ready to be crumpled and tossed into the trash along with the
    child and the table
a table as ridiculous as the drawing and as inconsistent as a
    child
when I saw the news on the internet about a homicide involving
    a child
I inferred that the child had drawn these sorts of landscapes
    that would drive
anyone crazy and push you into a state of such senselessness
that you can only get out of it by eliminating the drawing the
    child and you

amarte y odiarte es lo mismo porque no existes mi imaginación
    traza la imagen
de un monstruo yo amo al monstruo pero el monstruo me dejó
    sola en un aeropuerto
donde no caben ni mil pasajeros juntos fui al mercado y compré
    vísceras y no me pasaron
gato por liebre sino perro por carnero así que me comí el hígado
    de un perro que debió
ser gran danés labrador pitbull pastor alemán o dobermann lo
    hice a la italiana
con mucho pimiento y cebolla roja pero eso no quita que haya
    sido un golpe bajo
un trauma para mí que ya tenía suficiente con haber imaginado
    un monstruo y amarlo
y odiarlo con todas las fuerzas de mi propio hígado de perra
    lampiña si yo fuera
una perra de qué raza sería mirándolo bien sería un pekinés el
    perro más feo
que ojos humanos han visto Dios no me concedería la gracia de
    ser un can
de aeropuerto de esos que rastrean en los equipajes buscando
    ilícitas drogas
sería un pekinés y si algún día pisara un aeropuerto iría directo
    a ti y te mordería

hating you and loving you is all the same because you don't exist
    my imagination
sketches the image of a monster I love the monster but the
    monster left me alone in an airport
not big enough for even a thousand passengers I went to the
    market and bought innards and
I wasn't scammed but gutted so I ate the liver of a dog that must
have been a Great Dane lab pit bull German shepherd or
    Doberman I cooked it
Italian-style with lots of pepper and red onion but that doesn't
    mean it wasn't a low blow
a traumatic experience for me whose plate was already full
    what with imagining a monster
and loving it and hating it with all the might of my own liver of a
    hairless dog if I were
a dog what breed would I be at the end of the day I'd be a
    Pekingese the ugliest dog
ever seen with human eyes God wouldn't grant me the grace of
    being an airport
canine the kind that sniffs people's luggage for illegal drugs
I'd be a Pekingese and if I ever set foot in an airport I'd head
    straight for you and bite you

11

en glándulas mamarias el placer está presente lo sé tan bien
   como el péndulo
que se balancea sobre mí lo he sabido siempre y saberlo me hace
   libre me hace apta
en glándulas mamarias el dolor es un péndulo que se balancea
   sobre mí siempre
hasta ahora la muerte es lo más desagradable que conozco la
   muerte y la falta
de dinero lo demás se soluciona en días o no se soluciona nunca
   y se olvida
cuando se me ha ocurrido la idea de tirarme alante de un
   camión lo he olvidado
pero luego en las noticias veo que alguien lo hizo en mi lugar y
   ha sido escalofriante
la muerte no se olvida sigue dando vueltas en las sienes la falta
   de dinero no
se olvida en glándulas mamarias ni muerte ni falta de dinero
   placer y dolor sí
belleza y poesía son sinónimos el péndulo que se balancea me
   hace libre
con cuidado sobre mí me hace apta con cuidado si hay
   antecedentes familiares
negativos el cuerpo es susceptible a la repetición la mente
   obstaculiza tantos
pensamientos se prohíbe el consumo de licor de estrógeno y
   progesterona
se aconseja dar a luz y no ser de raza blanca ya fui libre y apta y
   ahora temo
se aconseja si es posible no besar no envejecer ya fui libre y apta
   y ahora temo

11

pleasure is present in mammary glands I know this as well as
    the pendulum
swinging overhead I've always known it it makes me free it
    makes me fit
for mammary glands pain is a pendulum always swinging
    overhead
thus far death is the most unpleasant thing I know death and the
    lack
of money everything else can be fixed in days or never fixed and
    then forgotten
whenever it's crossed my mind to step in front of a truck I've
    forgotten it
but then on the news I see that someone else did it instead and I
    find this chilling
death can't be forgotten it keeps whirling around in your
    temples the lack of money can't
be forgotten in mammary glands neither death nor the lack of
    money pleasure and pain can
beauty and poetry are synonyms the swinging pendulum sets
    me free
carefully overhead it makes me fit for care if there are negative
    precedents
in the family the body is susceptible to repetition the mind
    impedes so many
thoughts prohibits the consumption of liquor of estrogen and
    progesterone
advises itself to give birth and not be of the white race I once was
    free and fit and now I fear
it advises itself if possible not to kiss or grow old I once was free
    and fit and now I fear

22

fumamos en una pipa demasiado honda era tal vez un globo en
    forma de corazón
lo más hondo que te puedas imaginar y por tanto la yerba se
    perdía así que hicimos un
filtro con papel de chocolate extra puro y la yerba sabía a
    chocolate como el corazón
que sabe a chocolate almendrado y si es tu corazón tiene mil
    sabores al mismo tiempo
un corazón incomprensible debe ser el de un presidente
    cualquiera al azar toma
como ejemplo al presidente de los Estados Unidos de América y
    pruébalo a qué sabe
y no me lo digas basta mirar la expresión para saber a qué sabe
    para comprender
pues con este filtro logramos ahorrar bastante aquí está perdida
    y cuando se encuentra
hay que ahorrar mucho ahorrar siempre porque se acaba en un
    abrir y cerrar de ojos
y te quedas echado en la tierra baldía o en el mar de los sargazos
    o en un lecho de huesos
de piratas y corsarios perdón en un lecho de huesos de nuestros
    jóvenes caídos en combate
esos sí eran hombres de valía no los jóvenes de ahora la juventud
    también se ha perdido
me abandonaron es por eso que hablo tanto de flores yerba
    piratas presidentes

22

we smoked too deep a bowl maybe it was a heart-shaped
      balloon
the deepest thing you can imagine which meant the weed got
      lost in it so we made
a filter from an extra-dark chocolate wrapper and the weed
      tasted like chocolate like the heart
that tastes like almond chocolate and if it's your heart it tastes
      like a thousand things at once
the heart of any president must be completely incomprehensible
      take for instance
the president of the United States of America and see what it
      tastes like
and don't tell me all it takes is a glance at your face to know what
      it tastes like and understand
anyway using this filter we save quite a bit here it's *lost* and when
      it's found
you have to save a lot save always because it's all over in the
      blink of an eye
and you end up lying in a vacant lot or the sargasso sea or a bed
      of pirate
and corsair bones sorry on a bed of bones of our young men
      fallen in combat
now those were men of mettle not like young people today the
      youth is also *lost*
I was abandoned that's why I'm always going on about flowers
      weed pirates presidents

DE MIAMI CENTURY FOX[7]

FROM *MIAMI CENTURY FOX*

---

7   Brooklyn, NY: Akashic Books 2017. Winner of the Paz Poetry Prize, present-
    ed by the National Poetry Series and the Center for Writing and Literature at
    Miami Dade College.

¡Me planto!, grité.
Las manos amarillas de hepatitis.
Me voy por encima, dijo mamá,
y ganó el juego.

Fuji, Ararat

Mi amiga me lo dice por el chat.
Que tengo que quedarme, que es mejor.
Me dice que el amor no es el amor.
Yo creo en el amor. Se cae el chat.

Me voy al Monte Fuji, al Ararat.
Me tomo cuatro vasos de licor.
Me digo: ya verás que habrá confort,
no temas, pobre chica, little cat.

Vi un abismo, subiendo la colina.
Bajando la colina, vi un abismo.
¿Qué pasa si me pierdo en la neblina?

Cambiaré de sofá y metabolismo.
Cambiaré de laxante y aspirina.
Yo creo en el amor y en el turismo.

Stop! I yelled.
Hands yellowed with hepatitis.
I can beat that, said Mamá,
and won the game.

Fuji, Ararat

My friend gives me the news on Messenger.
She says I have to stay, it's for the best.
Besides, this loving isn't love, she says.
Me, I believe in love. Crash: there goes Messenger.

I travel to Mount Fuji, Ararat.
I guzzle down a drink, then three drinks more.
I tell myself: just wait, you'll see, there's succor
coming, don't be afraid, poor thing, sweet cat.

I saw a chasm as I climbed the hill.
And on my way back down, I saw a chasm.
What happens if I founder in the mist?

I'll change my sofa and metabolism.
I'll change the laxatives I take, the aspirin.
Me, I believe in love. And tourism.

Todas las fotos que quiero ver están en mi laptop.
Y si no, en mi teléfono.
Y si no, en Google. Y si no, en Facebook.
Y si no, en una nube.
¿Esas imágenes son reales, o falsas?

Mira la foto

No soy yo la que ríe en esa foto
ante el ojo perfecto que no eres.
Ni es la risa de mí lo que prefieres,
ni es la página seis la que se ha roto.

Cuando asoma mi pétalo de loto
es al pétalo al único que hieres.
Ten paciencia de árbol y no esperes
que me vaya y regrese, qué alboroto.

Luz y sombra, ternura y egoísmo
que me das y te doy, equivocada.
La foto de la luz provoca sismo.

Para ser una foto abandonada
tiene gracia mirarse en uno mismo
y ver del edificio la fachada.

All the photos I want to see are on my laptop.
Or else on my phone.
Or else on Google. Or else on Facebook.
Or else in a cloud.
Are these images real or fake?

I Look at the Picture

I'm not the person laughing in the picture
before the perfect eye that you are not.
It's not my laughter that you're wild about,
it's not the sixth page that has gone and ripped.

Look: when my lotus petal shows itself,
the petal is the only thing you bruise.
Be patient as a tree and don't suppose
I'll go away and then come back. A mess.

What you give me and I give you, mistaken,
are light and shadow, selfishness and care.
The photo of the light provokes a quake.

To be a photo thrown away, it's fun
to look as far as possible into your face,
discovering not the building but the front.

Entre mis cosas, cruzando el golfo,
un dispositivo externo con montones de películas.
Entre esas películas, Harmony Korine.
Él me muestra quién soy.
Y yo escribo quién soy.

Basura blanca

Más extraña que bus en la avenida
voy a pie por la acera de Le Jeune,
holgazana de todo y de ningún
trabajo. Tengo libros y una herida.

Más derecha que metro en la salida
serpenteo los autos, como atún
en profundos océanos. Algún
hombre sucio saluda. ¡Bienvenida!

Más ardilla que tren en el andén
subo por escalera horizontal
y me caigo de nalgas. Fuck you, *tren.*

Romerillo podrido en lodazal,
hormiguita dormida en su llantén,
cualquier cosa me sirve y me da igual.

Among my things, crossing the gulf,
an external device with scores of movies.
Among those movies, Harmony Korine.
He shows me who I am.
I write who I am.

White Trash

Far stranger than a sighting of the bus,
I make my way on foot along Le Jeune,
a jobless layabout of everything.
What I've got are some books, more books, a wound.

Far straighter than the subway on the out
I weave around the traffic like a deep-
sea tuna fish. Across the way, some greasy
fellow raises a hand to wave. Welcome!

Far squirrellier than an approaching train
I climb the horizontal stairs and plunge
ass-backward to the ground. I hate you, train.

A rotten blackjack blooming in the mud,
a tiny ant asleep among plantains,
I'll use whatever and don't give a fuck.

¿Un alien posee un ancestro?
¿Quién es el abuelo del alien?
En caso de ser un no-alien,
¿existe también un no-ancestro?

Ms Trolley recuerda países

Entonces, para no hacer largo el cuento
me dijeron su caso está aprobado
aunque es caso pendiente, delicado.
Y salí más tranquila, pero lento.

Desde cama/sofá, con desaliento,
recordé las ciudades donde he estado,
Mozambique, París, Tokio, Belgrado.
Solo en mapa y en sueños, no te miento.

Mi caso era un mal caso porque yo
tuviera la mirada que tuviera
tal vez decía sí cuando era no.

Y miraba a los ojos a cualquiera
porque fue lo que daddy *me enseñó*
seas alien o seas extranjera.

Does an alien have an ancestor?
Who is the alien's grandfather?
If it's a non-alien,
can it have a non-ancestor?

Ms. Trolley Remembers Countries

And so, to make a long story quite short,
they said *Congrats, your case has been approved,*
though it's still delicate, not yet defined.
And I left calmer, if slow on my feet.

A bit despondent on my sofa/bed,
I thought back to the cities I have known:
Paris, Mozambique, Belgrade, Tokyo.
Though just on maps and dreaming, I'll confess.

My case was a bad case because my eyes
said what they said no matter what I thought.
Maybe I meant a no when I said yes.

And I'd look anybody in the face,
just like my daddy always said to do
no matter what, foreign or alien.

La razón por la cual
continúo escribiendo sobre dígitos,
texturas, sentimientos,
es tan simple como la base de una familia,
una sociedad.
Esos procesos y yo, formamos una.

Once & Once

Once y once. Los dígitos iguales
significan iguales metonimias.
Ahora con qué rimo metonimias
si niego el diccionario. ¿Por qué sales

de adentro hacia más dentro? ¿Minerales?
Me da por recordar otras alquimias.
Alquimias solo rima con alquimias.
Once y once. Deshechos animales.

Next *dígito.* Next *piedra.* Next *tatuaje.*
Valora calidad de la llamada.
Mamita, ya no sigas con el viaje.

Once y once. O estás idiotizada,
o solo necesitas que el mensaje
atraviese el desierto y la nevada.

The reason why
I keep writing about digits,
textures, feelings,
is as simple as the foundation of a family,
a society.
These processes and I, we're one and the same.

Eleven & Eleven

Eleven and eleven. Equal digits
is tantamount to equal metonyms.
How am I supposed to rhyme with metonyms
if I reject the dictionary. What's

the point of leaving deep for deeper? Minerals?
I catch myself recalling other alchemies.
Nothing can rhyme with alchemies but alchemies.
Eleven and eleven. Waste from animals.

Next digit. Now next rock. Now next tattoo.
Please rate the sound quality of your call.
Mamita, time to come back from the cruise.

Eleven and eleven. You're a fool,
or else it's that you only need the text
to cross the desert and the fields of snow.

¿Qué pasa cuando uno decide destruir algo?
¿Y el hecho mismo de destrucción
en dónde nos coloca?
Pero cuando lo haces en el poema,
ahí sí, con seguridad,
habrá consecuencias.

Samantha murió

Colgamos a Samantha por el cuello
cuatro y veinte pasado meridiano.
Era triste su cuerpo tan enano
con un zapato feo y uno bello.

Samantha se llamaba, pero aquello
sonreía diabólico y freudiano,
y su par de pupilas de murano
envolvía en el último destello.

La colgamos así, sin programarlo,
de la ducha. La viga estaba floja.
Tuvimos que ponerlo y ajustarlo.

Por poco su vestido se le moja.
Samantha, corazón, hay que quitarlo.
Samantha se nos puso medio roja.

What happens when you decide to destroy something?
What about the act of destruction itself—
where does it leave us?
But when you do this in a poem,
surely there are bound
to be consequences.

Samantha's Dead

We hung Samantha by the neck at four
and twenty minutes in the afternoon.
Her tiny body made us sad to look
upon, with one ugly and one nice shoe.

Samantha, she was called, although that name
sounded somehow satanic, Freudian;
her pupils, glassy, practically Venetian,
encompassed in their spheres a final gleam.

We hung her there—we hadn't planned a thing—
inside the shower stall. The rod was loose.
We had to take it out, adjust the beam.

Along the way, her dress almost got wet.
Samantha, sweetheart, better take it off.
Samantha went a little red on us.

La Calle Ocho en Miami, histórica y trágica,
reúne a grupos foráneos que no me gustan.
Algo muy básico en la inteligencia emocional
de las personas: el gusto.
No me gustan.
Ni La Ocho.
Ni Flagler.
Ni las personas alrededor del lugar.
No me gustan, los repelo, están fuera del universo.

Second to your left, second to your right

En Jaguar amarillo hasta La Ocho
mirando al que me sigue por espejo,
fruncido el corazón y el entrecejo,
más múltiple que azúcar de bizcocho.

Hace un rato cumplí los dieciocho.
Me afeité los sobacos y el conejo.
Salí a desorientar, como un cangrejo,
en Jaguar amarillo hasta La Ocho.

Transeúnte, semáforo, Jaguar
avanza, retrocede, frena, corre.
Yo no sé si La Ocho es un lugar.

La cortina de humo se descorre.
Yo no sé si logré desorientar.
En La Ocho hay un niño y una torre.

La Calle Ocho in Miami, historic and tragic,
gathers together foreign groups I dislike.
It's a very basic thing in people's
emotional intelligence: taste.
I don't like them.
Or La Ocho.
Or Flagler.
Or the people around the place.
I don't like them, I repel them, they're outside the universe.

Second to Your Left, Second to Your Right

Driving a yellow Jaguar to La Ocho,
watching the car behind me in the mirror,
my heart and eyebrows scrunched into a furrow,
more multiple than grains of baking sugar.

I turned eighteen years old not long ago.
I oiled up my armpits and my pussy.
I went out with my crab-like plans to stray,
driving a yellow Jaguar to La Ocho.

Pedestrian, stoplight, the Jaguar revs,
advances and reverses, brakes and runs.
I'm not sure if La Ocho is a place.

The veil of smoke is parted and pulled back.
I'm not sure if I did manage to stray.
Along La Ocho there's a boy, a tower.

En español, existe una letra llamada ye,
conocida también como *i* griega.
Eso siempre me ha parecido curioso.
Y especial.
¿Te imaginas si cada letra
tuviera su propio país de origen?
¿Si cada una hubiera surgido
en una región diferente?

Delivery se escribe con i *griega*

Delivery *se escribe con* i *griega*
aunque sea italiana la comida.
Mi cara me parece conocida
aunque cuando la llamo nunca llega.

También Friday *se escribe con* i *griega,*
y el resto de las noches de mi vida.
Omega me parece conocida
aunque cuando la llamo no es Omega.

Lo que me está pasando es una tara
de familia con tiempo detenido.
La miro y no se mueve la cuchara.

Un hombre me parece conocido
pero ya no me gusta más su cara.
Hace más de diez Fridays *que se ha ido.*

In Spanish, there's a letter called ye,
or y, also known as the Greek i.
I've always found this strange.
And special.
Can you imagine if every letter
had its own country of origin?
If each one hailed
from a different region?

Delivery Is Spelled with the Greek *I*

Delivery is spelled with the Greek *i*
although the food you've ordered is Italian.
My face is recognizable to me,
although it never comes back when I call.

Friday is also spelled with the Greek *i*,
like all the other nights I've come to know.
Omega strikes me as familiar, though
it's not Omega when I call its name.

What's happening to me is just a fault
of family with time stopped all around.
I look at it. The spoon declines to move.

I think I recognize a man whose face,
it now turns out, I don't like anymore.
It's been ten Fridays since that man's been gone.

DE MI PAREJA CALVA Y YO VAMOS A TENER UN HIJO[8]

FROM *MY BALD GIRLFRIEND AND I ARE GOING TO HAVE A BABY*

8   Cáceres: Ediciones Liliputienses, 2019. A jury composed of Aníbal Cristobo, Berta García Faet, Juan Carlos Mestre, Miriam Reyes, and Ballerina Vargas Tinajero awarded the Second Centrifugados Prize for young poets to *Mi pareja calva y yo vamos a tener un hijo*.

La emoción de orinar sobre un test de embarazo

Es la misma emoción de saber que has tomado
Tus propias decisiones con tu propia conciencia.

No te pesan los brazos ni te pesan los hombros
Y mientras el orine empapa la rosada
Durante aquellos cinco segundos en el mundo
Solo hay tensión ahí
Mi uretra y yo son una.

Mi novia, la otra madre, espera en la cocina.
Yo salgo del lavabo.
La abrazo.
Ve a mirar.
Lo siento, es negativo.

Pero no es negativo.
Hay una línea tenue.
Tan tenue como el miedo a orinar
Otra vez.

The Feeling of Peeing on a Pregnancy Test

Is the same feeling as knowing you've made
Your own informed decisions.

Your arms and shoulders don't weigh you down
And as the urine soaks the pink strip
For those five seconds in the world
There's only tension there
My urethra and I are one.

My girlfriend, the other mother, waits in the kitchen.
I emerge from the bathroom.
I hug her.
She goes to look.
I'm sorry, it's negative.

But it's not negative.
There's a faint line.
As faint as the fear of peeing
Again.

Louise Glück soñaba

Louise Glück soñaba.
Tuve una abuela tocaya de Louise Glück.
Pero en español.
Y esa también soñaba.

Muchas veces me llamó en sueños y yo acudí.
Cuando una abuela llama, acudir es lo menos que puedes hacer.
Aunque en la vida real cuando me llamó no lo hice.

Tal vez estaba lejos.

Me queda la duda de cuál vida sigo.
Si la real o la del sueño.

Cada vez que me despierto estoy tirándole piedras a las
Puertas de cristal del Dolphin Mall.
Luego viene un policía a pedirme documentos.

Pero el policía no cree que Averno,
Un libro de Louise Glück que siempre cargo en mi mochila,
Sea ningún documento de identidad.

Louise Glück Dreamed

Louise Glück dreamed.
One of my grandmothers had the same name as Louise Glück.
But in Spanish.
And she dreamed too.

She often called to me in dreams, and I went.
When a grandmother calls, going is the least you can do.
Although in real life when she called to me I never did.

Maybe she was far away.

I'm left with the question of which life I follow.
My real life or the dream life.

Every time I wake up, I'm throwing rocks at the
Glass doors of the Dolphin Mall.
Then a cop comes and asks for my documents.

But the cop doesn't believe that *Averno*,
A book by Louise Glück I always carry in my backpack,
Is any kind of official ID.

El hijo y el hada

La librería donde trabajo es venezolana.
Los dueños de la librería son venezolanos.
La sección de libros venezolanos está a la derecha.
Los clientes venezolanos compran libros venezolanos
De fotos venezolanas y comida venezolana
Y biografías venezolanas de venezolanos insignes.

Casi todos los días me compro un libro y cuando llego a casa leo
       en voz alta
A ver si mi acento sigue siendo el mismo
O ya cambió.

De donde vengo le decimos "plásticas" sobre todo a las artes.

En tiempo de lluvias caen goteras
Y debo poner el "plástico" para proteger los libros.

Los chinos han inventado cierto tipo de arroz "plástico" y de
       lechuga "plástica".
He visto los videos en YouTube.
Eso no es arte.

Si mi embrión crece, se desarrolla y nace
Soy capaz de eliminar todo el "plástico" del mundo.

The Son and the Fairy

The bookstore where I work is Venezuelan.
The owners of the bookstore are Venezuelan.
The Venezuelan book section is to the right.
The Venezuelan customers buy Venezuelan books
Of Venezuelan photos and Venezuelan food
And Venezuelan biographies of illustrious Venezuelans.

I buy myself a book almost every day and when I get home
        I read aloud
To see if my accent is holding steady
Or has changed.

Where I come from, it's art we call "plastic" more than
        anything else.

When it rains, there are leaks
And I apply "plastic" to protect the books.

The Chinese have invented a certain kind of "plastic"
        rice and "plastic" lettuce.
I've seen the YouTube videos.
That's not art.

If my embryo grows, develops, and is born,
I'll be capable of eliminating all the "plastic" in the world.

Palabras y números

¿Puedes oírlo?
Preguntó la enfermera
Volteando hacia mí
El monitor cuadrado.

Yo podía oírlo
Y verlo
Hacía igual que mi corazón
Pero no era mi corazón
No era nada que yo pudiera asociar
Con ninguna cosa conocida hasta ahora.

Pensé en las palabras
Que conozco hasta ahora
No son muchas
A veces las escribo mal
Y me avergüenzo.

Pensé en los números
Tampoco muchos
Y también los escribo mal
Aunque no me avergüenzo.

Cualquier elemento sublime de mi vida
Ha dejado de serlo para siempre.

Words and Numbers

Can you hear that?
The nurse asked
Turning the square monitor
Toward me.

I could hear it
And see it
It sounded like just like my heart
But it wasn't my heart
It wasn't anything I could associate
With anything else I'd ever known.

I thought of all the words
I've ever known
There aren't many
Sometimes I misspell them
And feel ashamed.

I thought of the numbers
Not many either
And I miswrite them too
But don't feel ashamed.

Any sublime element of my own life
Has stopped being one forever.

Cemí

Te hemos visto balbuceando
En el útero.
Dando vueltas de carnero
Y contorsiones preciosas.

Te hemos mirado bien.
Cómo explicarte
Que tienes dos madres
En vez de una.

Que según la ciencia
Eres un varón
Y que a mí no me hizo falta
Ninguna ciencia
Para saberlo.

Que las semanas
Pasan volando
Y tu nombre es tuyo
Desde la semana nueve.

Cómo explicar tu nombre
Sobre una pila de nombres
Desechados
Y saber que tu nombre
Te representa
Ante el mundo
Lo mismo
Que ante nosotras.

Dame fuerzas para explicarlo todo
Y para hacerme entender
Al menos lo necesario.

Cemí

We've seen you babbling
In utero.
Turning somersaults,
A beautiful contortionist.

We've watched you closely.
How to explain
That you have two mothers
Instead of one.

That science defines you
As a boy
And I needed
No science
To know it.

That the weeks
Fly past
And your name has been yours
Since week nine.

How to explain your name
Atop a pile of discarded
Names
And know that your name
Represents you
Before the world
As it does
Before the two of us.

Give me the strength to explain it all
And let me understand
At least the basics.

El país que uno habita nunca es un país

Me explico:
Cuando somos muy jóvenes
Creemos que el país son los amigos
A menudo tenemos amigos grandes
Mayores que nosotros en edad y altura
Y esos son los amigos que más queremos
Y hacemos hasta lo imposible
Por estar cerca de ellos
Y tratamos de ser importantes para ellos
Y tratamos de ser alguien.

Después pasan los años
Pero aun somos tan jóvenes
Como para marcar diferencias
Entonces creemos que el país son esos novios
O novias
De los cuales nos enamoramos
Siempre para siempre
Y hacemos hasta lo imposible
Por estar cerca de ellos
Y tratamos de ser importantes para ellos
Y tratamos de ser alguien.

Siguen pasando los años ahora sí parecemos otra cosa
Bien suficiente y bien contundente
Y dejamos de creer en casi todo
Menos en algo que sigue siendo
Más o menos un país.

Me explico:
El único país que tú y yo defenderíamos
Por el único que daríamos la nuca

The Country You Live in Is Never a Country

Let me explain:
When we're very young
We think a country means our friends
Many of our friends are older
And taller than we are
And those friends are our favorites
And we do the impossible
To be near them
And we try to be important for them
And we try to be someone.

Then years pass
But we're still too young
To mark any differences
So we believe that a country means the boyfriends
Or girlfriends
We fall in love with
Forever always forever
And we do the impossible
To be near them
And we try to be important for them
And we try to be someone.

The years keep passing now we do seem different
Convincing and enough
And we stop believing in almost everything
Except for something that remains
More or less a country.

Let me explain:
The only country you and I would ever defend
The only one we'd put our hands in the fire for

Sería el pequeño hombre
Que llevo dentro de mí
Con dos fémures de diecinueve semanas
Y dos hemisferios iguales
En la cabeza.

Is the little man
Inside me
With two nineteen-week-old femurs
And two equal hemispheres
In his head.

El hombre de mi vida

Todas somos mujeres en la casa
La casa también es una mujer
Las puertas y las ventanas
La gata y la perra
La luna allá afuera
La droga de los vecinos
Que vuela bajo la luna
Y entra por la ventana
Y me da náusea
La náusea también es una mujer.

Todas somos mujeres en la casa
Todas nos orinamos
Si aguantamos mucho las ganas
La novia entra a la casa
La gata sale a la yerba
La perra sale a la tierra
Desde la casa hasta la tierra
Todo es una mujer
La gana también es una mujer.
Alguna vez deseé
Cierto elemento que fuera
Diferente.
El pensamiento no es una mujer
Y el deseo tampoco.

Es obvio que se formara esto
En mis entrañas
Y que creciera tanto
Y que al verlo pesar apenas medio kilo
Me hiciera olvidar la casa
La tierra
Y la náusea.

The Man of My Life

We're all women in this house
The house is also a woman
The windows and doors
The cat and the dog
The moon outside
The neighbors' drugs
That fly under the moon
And waft in through the window
And make me nauseous
Nausea is also a woman.

We're all women in this house
We all piss ourselves
If we hold it in too long
The girlfriend comes into the house
The cat goes out to the grass
The dog goes out to the dirt
From the house to the earth
It's all a woman
Lust is also a woman.
Once I longed
For some element that would be
Different.
Thinking isn't a woman
And desire isn't either.

It's obvious that this would be formed
Deep inside me
And grow so much
That when I saw it weighed just a pound
It would make me forget all about the house
The dirt
And the nausea.

La barriga

Frente al Mississippi
No se me notaba la barriga.

En el Motel de 75 dólares la noche
no se me notaba la barriga.

Junto a la estatua de José Martí
Con la que chocamos por casualidad
No se me notaba la barriga.

En la casa de William Faulkner
Donde me quedé fría y tiesa
Mi barriga era nada.

Con 7 grados centígrados
Parece que la barriga se esconde.

La única sopa que pude tomarme
Fue de cangrejo
Y la barriga no se dio por enterada.

Mojando un tibio beignet
En una taza de Café Du Monde
La barriga se salió un poquito
Pero nadie la vio.

Ya en el parque sobre la hierba
Goloseando unas toronjas como pelotas de fútbol
Escuché un murmullo de lo alto.

Era Mahalia Jackson
contándole algún chisme al trompetista:

The Belly

Facing the Mississippi River
My belly didn't show.

In the 75-dollar-a-night motel
My belly didn't show.

Beside the statue of José Martí
We bumped into by accident
My belly didn't show.

At William Faulkner's house
Where I went cold and stiff
My belly was nothing.

At 45 degrees Fahrenheit
It's like the belly hides.

The only soup I could eat
Was crab soup
And my belly didn't notice.

Dipping a warm beignet
Into a cup at Café du Monde
My belly stuck out a little
But no one saw.

Sitting in the grass in the park
Savoring a grapefruit great as a soccer ball
I heard a murmur from on high.

It was Mahalia Jackson
Gossiping with the trumpet player:

"¿Viste eso, Louis?,
La muchacha que acaba de pasar
En vez de uno, tiene dos corazones".

"See that, Louis?
The girl who just walked by
Has two hearts, not one."

INÉDITOS

UNPUBLISHED POEMS

Mis senos son mellizos y se llaman garlic roll

Se parecen
pero no son iguales
y eso nos pasa a todas
querramos o no querramos
desde que nacemos
y hasta que morimos
los muy deliciosos
solo se parecen.
Por mucho que los arregles
o los expongas a cirugías
nunca llegan a ser iguales
se parecen
pero son distintos
y eso nos pasa a todas.
De pie ante el espejo
estamos todas
mirándonos esas fuentes
a los cinco años.
De pie ante el espejo
estamos todas
poniendo el dedito
a los doce años.
De pie ante el espejo
estamos todas
rompiendo el espejo
con la cabeza.

Hoy mi espejo es una plancha
y mi cabeza un ladrillo
y no digo que sí
ni que no
porque al inclinarme

My Breasts Are Twins and Their Name Is Garlic Roll

They look alike
but they're not the same
and that happens to all of us
no matter what
from birth
to death
these delicious things
only look alike.
No matter how you fix them up
or subject them to surgeries
they'll never be the same
they look alike
but they're different
and that happens to all of us.
Standing in front of the mirror
we all stare
at those fountains
at age five.
Standing in front of the mirror
we all slip
a finger in
at age twelve.
Standing in front of the mirror
we all
crack the mirror
with our heads.

Today my mirror is an iron
and my head's a brick
and I don't say either yes
or no
because when I lean forward

para limpiar la plancha
los aplasto
contra las costillas.
Es el único momento
en que de igual forma
sangran
fuera de ahí
jamás son iguales.
Toma una al azar
desnúdala y mírala
verás que presenta un par
delicioso y voluminoso
que constituye anomalía.
Toma una al azar
y no te la comas
hasta que veas
la extravagancia
no te la comas
aunque se alteren
tus papilas.
Algunas desarrollan
tan ínfimo crecimiento
que se les confunde
con varón
lo que las atormenta
o hace felices
en caso de inconformidad
o en caso de orgullo
respectivamente.
Otras desarrollan
un crecimiento excedido
lo que socialmente impacta
y profesionalmente importa.
El cumplimiento del deber
será sin duda un éxito

to wash the pan
I crush them
against my ribs.
It's the only time
when they bleed
equally
otherwise
they're never the same.
Choose one at random
bare it and take a good look
you'll see it reveals
a delicious and voluminous pair
that constitutes an anomaly.
Choose one at random
and don't eat it
until you see
the extravagance
don't eat it
even if your taste buds
get flustered.
Some grow
so negligibly
that they're mistaken
for boys
which haunts them
or thrills them
in cases of displeasure
or pride
respectively.
Others grow
in great excess
with striking social
and significant professional consequences.
The fulfillment of duty
will be a certain success

aunque no sean iguales
aunque solo se parezcan.
Otras los pierden
en el camino
a veces ambos
a veces uno
en caso de ser uno
su hermano lo extrañará
sin consuelo.
Mi humilde experiencia
se caracteriza
por una hipersensibilidad espontánea
y un tamaño propio
de sangre infantil
que no quita el deterioro
ni los exonera
del afeamiento.
Quien haya visto el panorama
dará fe.
Quien haya tocado y visto
dará fe.
Quien haya probado y visto
asentirá sin mover cabeza
o morder labio.

even if they're not the same
even if they only look alike.
Others lose them
along the way
sometimes both
sometimes one
if it's just one
its brother will miss it
inconsolably.
My humble experience
is characterized
by a spontaneous hypersensitivity
and a size befitting
the blood of a child
that doesn't exempt them from deterioration
or exonerate them
from progressive ugliness.
Anyone who has seen the view
will attest to it.
Anyone who has touched and seen
will attest to it.
Anyone who has tasted and seen
will agree without nodding their head
or biting their lips.

Mc Donald contra Pollo Tropical

Las mujeres que trabajan
codo a codo conmigo
siempre comen afuera.
El grupo es impar
pero así y todo
se divide en dos
unas entran a Mc Donald
otras entran
a Pollo Tropical.
No sé dónde come el manager
pero nunca lo he visto
atravesando puertas
ni de Pollo Tropical
ni de Mc Donald.
Las puertas
que atraviesa un manager
permanecen a la sombra
de árboles antiguos
o rascacielos.
Codo a codo conmigo
viene mamá
queriendo atravesar
la puerta de Mc Donald
para quitarse la picazón.
Codo a codo conmigo
viene papá
queriendo atravesar
la puerta de Mc Donald
para chuparse los dedos.
Codo a codo conmigo
viene un haitiano
pidiéndome dinero

McDonald's vs. Pollo Tropical

The women who work
shoulder to shoulder with me
always go out for lunch.
It's an odd-numbered group
but even so
it splits in two
some go to McDonald's
some go
to Pollo Tropical.
I don't know where the manager eats
but I've never seen him
walking through the doors
of either Pollo Tropical
or McDonald's.
The doors
a manager walks through
remain in the shade
of ancient trees
or skyscrapers.
Shoulder to shoulder with me
comes Mamá
wanting to walk through
the McDonald's doors
to scratch an itch.
Shoulder to shoulder with me
comes Papá
wanting to walk through
the McDonald's doors
to lick his fingers.
Shoulder to shoulder with me
comes a Haitian guy
asking me for money

y amor.
Lo empujo contra la puerta
de Pollo Tropical
y el haitiano sale más limpio
que como entró.
Lo empujo contra Mc Donald
y el haitiano sale tieso
el blanco de sus ojos
tiene salsa de tomate.
Me olvido de la importancia
de la poesía
y también de la importancia
de la ciencia
Mc Donald se ha convertido
en un país natal.
Las mujeres que nacen en Mc Donald
defienden su idiosincrasia
y no entran a Pollo Tropical.
Así mismo las que nacen
en Pollo Tropical
defienden su doctrina
y no entran a Mc Donald.
El manager no tiene
adoctrinamiento
por eso es un hombre
que ha triunfado.
Por más que mi doctrina
sea la de las esponjas
todavía no he triunfado.
Y por más que me atraigan
cierto tipo de puertas
impulsándome fuerte
hacia ellas
con toda la intención
de atravesarlas

and love.
I push him against the door
of Pollo Tropical
and the Haitian guy comes out cleaner
than when he went in.
I push him against McDonald's
and he comes out stiff
and the whites of his eyes
have tomato sauce in them.
I forget all about the importance
of poetry
and also the importance
of science
McDonald's has become
a native country.
The women born in McDonald's
defend its idiosyncrasy
and don't go to Pollo Tropical.
Likewise, the women born
in Pollo Tropical
defend its doctrine
and don't go to McDonald's.
No matter how much my doctrine
may be the doctrine of sponges,
I haven't triumphed yet.
And no matter how attracted
I may be to certain doors,
propelling myself forcefully
in their direction
with every intent
to cross them,
I haven't triumphed yet.
I can still see
the populations
moving back and forth

todavía no he triunfado.
Aún puedo ver
a las poblaciones
moviéndose de un lado
al otro de la calle.
Las veo desde mi querido
país natal.
Como buena trabajadora
yo también como afuera
les digo hasta mañana
y atravieso la puerta
de un Liquor Store.

across the street.
I can see them from my beloved
native country.
Like every good worker
I also go out for lunch
I say see you tomorrow
and walk right
into a liquor store.

Junta las manos a la altura del pecho,
inclina la cabeza levemente hacia abajo,
cierra los ojos, abre la boca

Virgen de La Caridad del Cobre
Santa María de la Caridad
que viniste a nosotros
sobre las aguas
con agua en los oídos
con espinas de paz
eres mi madre
la madre de todos
nosotros juntos
tengo una vela
en la garganta.
A ti acudimos
para honrar la fuente
que se te rompió
tan rota y simple
como divina
mi amor es el amor
de un hijo huérfano.
Tu corazón de madre
es todo lo que queremos
a nosotros nos hicieron
un trasplante de corazón.
Ni ansias ni esperanzas
ni afanes ni súplicas
a ti acudimos
para que entiendas
que eres mi madre
la madre de todos
nosotros juntos.
Eres más mujer que hombre

Press Your Hands Together at Chest-Height, Bow Your Head Slightly, Close Your Eyes, Open Your Mouth

Our Lady of La Caridad del Cobre
Holy Mary of Charity
who came to us
over the waters
with water in your ears
with thorns of hope
you're my mother
the mother of all
of us together
I have a candle
in my throat.
We turn to you
to honor the platter
you broke
as simple and broken
as it is divine
my love is the love
of an orphaned child.
Your mother's heart
is all we want
we received
a heart transplant.
Neither angst nor hope
neither zeal nor pleas
we turn to you
to make you understand
that you're my mother
the mother of all
of us together.
You're more woman than man

y más hombre que mujer
por tus cojones de madre
nacieron hijos libérrimos.
La patria de tus hijos
te da la bienvenida
si nos quedamos sin patria
vuelve al mar
y constitúyela.
Mi familia
te da la bienvenida
no dejes que una familia
se separe en pedazos
los niños de la familia
han dejado de crecer.
Nunca serán jóvenes
o probablemente
nunca volverán a ser
nada
a nosotros nos hicieron
un trasplante de corazón.
La enfermedad y la marginalidad
pertenecen al presente
y nosotros no existimos
mi corazón
se llama futuro.
La iglesia
donde tus hijos asisten
tiene un sacerdote
con doscientas
caras felices
su último mensaje
fue un signo de dos puntos
seguido de un punto y coma
significa que nos hacía
un guiño.

and more man than woman
your mother's balls
birthed children free as birds.
Your children's homeland
welcomes you
if we're left without a homeland
then return to the sea
and constitute it.
My family
welcomes you
don't let a family
shatter into pieces
the family's children
have stopped growing.
They'll never be young
or probably
will never be anything
ever again
we received
a heart transplant.
Disease and marginalization
belong to the present
and we don't exist
my heart
is called the future.
The church
your children attend
has a priest
with two hundred
happy faces
his last message
was a colon
followed by a semicolon
it means he was winking
at us.

Bendice mi iglesia
madre santísima.
La justicia sin victoria
tampoco logra existencia
hazme victorioso
y amistoso con los pueblos.
Tengo montones
de hermanos regados
en cada pueblo del mundo.
Esos también son tus hijos
fuiste muy fértil mamá.
Bendita tú eres
porque ya eres
sobre un oleaje
de mar rabioso
mátanos madre
en cuanto tengas
la más mínima oportunidad
la necesidad de un corazón
nos puede dar por cualquier cosa.
A nosotros la gloria
y el poder.

Bless my church
holy mother.
Justice without victory
doesn't secure existence either
make me victorious
and friendly with all peoples.
I have tons
of brothers scattered
across all the peoples of the world.
They're your children too
you were very fertile, mamá.
Bless you
for already you rise
over the surf
of a furious sea
kill us, mother
at the slightest
opportunity
the need for a heart
may strike us at any moment.
Glory and power
unto us.

Una gata

Lo que hago con la poesía es tapar la mierda.
Tapo y tapo. Con las manos. Con los pies.
Como un gato o una gata que no presta atención.

A Cat

What I do with poetry is cover up the shit.
I cover and cover it. With my hands. With my feet.
Like a cat that ignores you.

Huracán leña

Me fui a vivir sola con mi hijo de 36 meses
en una ciudad donde la gente vive en pareja para poder pagar
     las facturas.
Me compré un carrito Chevy Spark Místico azul del año
     que pago a base de cuotas
en una ciudad donde la gente compra carritos grises negros
     blancos o rojos
y casi nunca del año para no tener que pagar cuotas.
Conseguí una perra mixta Beagle en Craigslist Miami
como si tuviera un patio o un pedazo de cemento
donde la perra pudiera hacer sus necesidades
en una ciudad donde la gente adopta gatos
porque dizque los gatos son de adorno.
Me enamoré de una mujer que vive en Cuba.
Alguien puede decirme cómo se llega a Cuba.
Si me preguntan Where do you live
siempre respondo con la mirada.
Me puse a pensar que cualquier día podría
convertirme en huracán
e irme volando con hijo y todo
cuando tomara una curva alta desde una Interestatal.
En eso pensaba cuando de pronto
salí volando con hijo y todo
en una ciudad donde lo que vuela
aterriza rápido.

Hurricane Leña

I went to live alone with my thirty-six-month-old son
in a city where people live as couples so they can pay the bills.
I bought a new mystic blue Chevy Spark I pay off in
     installments
in a city where people buy gray black white or red cars
and almost never new ones so they don't have to pay in
     installments.
I found a beagle mix on the Miami Craigslist
as if I had a yard or a square of cement
where the dog could do her business
in a city where people adopt cats
because cats are supposedly decorative.
I fell in love with a woman who lives in Cuba.
Can someone please tell me how to get to Cuba.
When asked *Where do you live*
I always answer with my eyes.
I started thinking that any day now I could
turn into a hurricane
and fly away son and all
whenever I take a high curve on the interstate.
That's what I was thinking about when all of a sudden
I flew away son and all
in a city where everything that flies
is quick to land.

A mi mujer

El verdadero prejuicio
consiste
en decirle a una mujer
que se parece a un hombre
por decirle a su novia
que se quite ese short
ahora mismo
que no salga
para la calle
así.
¿Quién dijo
que mandar a quitar un short
es cosa solo de hombres
posesivos
primitivos?
¿Entonces una mujer
no puede querer para sí
lo que es de ella
y seguir siendo
únicamente
tan mujer
como Kate Winslet
Juliette Binoche
o Gatúbela?
A veces he visto árboles
tapando a la luna
y viceversa.
¿A quién se le ocurre
que despreciar
a todas las mujeres
que te rodean

To My Wife

The true prejudice
is to tell
a woman
she's like a man
because she told her girlfriend
to take off those shorts
right now
not to go
out
like that.
Who ever said
that telling someone to take off their shorts
is the sole dominion
of primitive
possessive men?
So a woman
can't want to have what's hers
all to herself
and keep being
exclusively
as much a woman
as Kate Winslet
Juliette Binoche
or Gatúbela?
Sometimes I've seen trees
covering the moon
and vice versa.
Who would think
that scorning
all the women
around you

no es lo más sublime
que yo haya sentido
jamás?

isn't the most magnificent thing
I've ever
felt?

Una isla rodeada de filología por todas partes

Ahora. Mismo. Hay. Un hombre leyendo Paradiso,
de Lezama, y Corrección, *de Thomas Bernhard, a la vez.*
Los lee quieto, sin que el hecho de leer constituya adaptación.
Tiene la garganta enferma, le dan escalofríos de noche.
Se fue de Cuba. Vive en Miami Beach.
Que no es Miami, pero ideológicamente sí.
Sus lecturas simultáneas forman parte de algún virus.
Miel para la garganta, duralginas y miel.
Al contrario de la duralgina le preocupa la novela
de Lezama: solo he conseguido llegar al tercer capítulo.
Le he dicho que abandone Paradiso, *que continúe*
con Thomas. Me responde que no abandonará.
Cada mensaje de texto mide unas pocas bimembres:
El lector-simulador sirviendo descafeinados.
Al rato me refiero a Cuba como: una isla
rodeada de filología por todas partes.
Según el lector enfermo ese podría ser
el título de mi próximo libro.
Hablamos. Por escrito. Durante
media hora sobre el lenguaje.
Él piensa que, a diferencia de Thomas
Bernhard, Lezama Lima es lenguaje.
Yo pienso que, a diferencia del lenguaje, Thomas
Bernhard es lenguaje. Lezama es filología.

An Island Surrounded by Philology on All Sides

Right. Now. There. Is. A man reading *Paradiso*,
by Lezama Lima, and *Correction*, by Thomas Bernhard, at the
    same time.
He sits still as he reads. The act of reading doesn't constitute
    adaptation.
His throat is sick, he shivers at night.
He left Cuba. He lives in Miami Beach.
Which isn't Miami, except for ideologically.
His simultaneous readings are part of a virus.
Honey for the throat, codeine and honey.
Unlike the codeine, Lezama Lima's novel
perturbs him: he's only made it to chapter three.
I've told him to abandon *Paradiso* and press on
with Thomas. He tells me he won't abandon it.
Each text message encompasses two subjects:
the reader-simulator pouring decaf.
I soon refer to Cuba as: an island
surrounded by philology on all sides.
The sick reader thinks that this could be
the title of my next book.
We talk. In writing. For
half an hour about language.
He thinks that, unlike Thomas
Bernhard, Lezama Lima is language.
I think that, unlike language, Thomas
Bernhard is language. Lezama Lima is philology.

El punto cubano

Estuve días soñando con los muertos que más quiero.
Soñé con todos mis perros que se murieron de noche.
Soñé con todos aquellos que se murieron de hambre.
Yo tuve un perro llamado Mickey Mouse como el ratón.
Ese murió envenenado en el patio entre las matas.
Se comió todo el veneno que mi papá le había echado
a las más de cien millones de cucarachas que había.
Soñé con un hemofílico que fue mi novio en primaria.
Teníamos siete años y nos queríamos mucho
pero él se murió chiquito porque su sangre era mala.
Soñé con todos los gatos que me comí sin saberlo.
Era un período difícil, papá tuvo que matarlos.
Venía con esos gatos descuerados en su bolso
y le decía a mi abuela que eran pollos o conejos,
y mi abuela simulaba que eran pollos o conejos,
y mi madre simulaba que eran pollos o conejos,
y yo solo me comía la carne deliciosísima
con harina de maíz o con boniato picado.
Soñé con mi abuela mora más de cien días, más días
de los que nunca he soñado con cualquier cosa querible.
Soñé también con mi abuelo, el cascarrabia español
que me crió y me llevaba a la escuela en un caballo.
El esposo de la mora, pero no moro. Galicia
fue la tierra de su madre, otra vieja cascarrabia.
Se llamaba Ángel Iglesias Novoa, para servirle.
Usaba un sombrero alón igualito al de Camilo.

Camilo fue un héroe bueno que mataron por reírse.
El avión donde ellos iban se cayó por Camagüey.
Desde entonces en octubre echamos flores al mar.

El Punto Cubano

I dreamed for days of the dead I loved most.
I dreamed of all my dogs that died at night.
I dreamed of all the ones that starved to death.
I had a dog named Mickey Mouse, like the cartoon.
He was poisoned to death in the yard, among the weeds.
He ate all the poison that my dad had set out
for the more than hundred million cockroaches out there.
I dreamed of the hemophiliac who was my elementary school
    boyfriend.
We were seven years old and loved each other very much
but he died young because his blood was bad.
I dreamed of all the cats I ate unwittingly.
It was a difficult time, Papá had to kill them.
He showed up with all those skinned cats in a bag
and told my grandmother that they were chickens or rabbits,
and my grandmother pretended they were chickens or rabbits,
and my mother pretended they were chickens or rabbits,
and all I did was eat the succulent meat
with corn flour or cubed sweet potato.
I dreamed of my Moorish grandmother for over a hundred
    days, more days
than I've ever dreamed of any lovable thing.
I also dreamed of my grandfather, the grouchy Spaniard
who raised me and took me to school on horseback.
La Mora's husband, but no Moro. Galicia
was the homeland of his mother, another old grouch.
His name was Ángel Iglesias Novoa, at your service.
He wore an alón hat like Camilo Cienfuegos.

Camilo was a good hero they killed for laughing.
Their plane went down over Camagüey.
Every October ever since, we toss flowers into the sea.

Pero en verdad lo mataron con un disparo de gracia.
En mi sueño casi nada parecía tener lógica.
Era lógico mi sueño, pero no que lo soñara.
Yo estaba muy temblorosa, quiero decir, en el sueño.
Debía decirle al hombre lo que venía a decirle.
Un hombre que había sido más comunista que Marx
y más marxista que Marx cuando Marx era un buen tipo.
Que todavía lo era, más comunista que el muro
antes de ser derribado, mucho más que cualquier muro.
Ese hombre era mi abuelo pero en el sueño era solo
un hombre súper extraño mirándose los zapatos.
Toda la noche frotando los zapatos con betún.
Así pasaban los hombres sus noches y sus mañanas.
Frotándolos con un paño embarrado de betún.
A mí me gustaba eso, yo también froté los míos
para ir a la escuela limpia y lustrada, con mi abuelo.
La del sueño no sabía cómo enunciar el mensaje.
La de afuera que era yo no la podía ayudar.
¿Cómo le digo a mi abuelo que una tarde parí un yankee?
¿Sentados en otomanes y llorando en octosílabos,
frente a una pared vacía a la que da el sol de frente?
En otra época el sol me parecía un insulto
y las paredes, por Dios, eran hombres sin vergüenza.
Entonces mi abuelo dijo: ¡si serás desvergonzada!
A lo que yo interrogué: ¿no querrías conocerlo?
Después la tarde siguió hacia un sendero de dudas.
Es solo un ser diminuto, su mollera sigue abierta,
amar a un hermoso yankee *no será nunca traición.*
¿Cómo le digo a mi abuelo que una tarde parí un yankee?
Que no fue naturalmente sino cesárea de urgencia
porque su ritmo cardíaco empezó a disminuir
y el obstetra entró de pronto y me dijo: hay que sacarlo.

But they actually killed him with a coup de grâce.
Almost nothing was especially logical in my dream.
My dream was logical, but not what I dreamed.
I should have told the man what I'd come to tell him.
A man who'd been more communist than Marx
and more Marxist than Marx when Marx was a good guy.
Which he still was, more communist than the wall
before it came down, much more communist than any wall.
That man was my grandfather, but in my dream he was just
a strange man looking down at his shoes.
Rubbing his shoes with polish all night long.
That's how men spent their nights and their mornings.
Rubbing them with a towel coated in polish.
I liked that, and I rubbed mine too
so I'd show up clean and shiny at school, with my grandfather.
The girl in the dream didn't know how to phrase the message.
The girl outside who was me couldn't help her.
How can I tell my grandfather that I gave birth to a Yankee one
    evening?
Sitting on ottomans and weeping in octosyllables,
facing a bare wall that the sun hit head-on?
In another time, I found the sun insulting,
and the walls, by God, were shameless men.
Then my grandfather said: aren't you shameless!
To which I demanded: don't you want to meet him?
Then the afternoon proceeded along a path of doubt.
He's just a tiny being, his skull's still open,
loving a beautiful Yankee will never be a betrayal.
How to tell my grandfather that I gave birth to a Yankee one
    evening?
That it wasn't a natural birth, but an emergency C-section,
because his heartbeat started to slow
and the obstetrician burst in and said: we've got to get him out.

¿Cómo le digo a mi abuelo que el niño nació en Miami
y que vivirá en Miami y que crecerá en Miami
y que no hablará español, sino espanglish, un idioma
de bárbaros, de campeones, de familias de emigrantes?
¿Cómo le digo a mi abuelo que me he vuelto una emigrante?
Entonces mi abuelo dijo: tráeme a tu hijo, vejiga.
Y yo le traje a mi hijo envuelto en mi propia blusa,
desnudito, dormidito, en el sueño hacía aire.
Mi abuelo tomó al muchacho por los pies, dándole vueltas,
yo gritaba horrorizada, yo me iba a morir del susto.
Si sobrevive, es mi nieto, dijo mi abuelo mareado.
El muchacho abrió los ojos un par de veces, ¡me muero!
El muchacho estaba vivo y tenía tanta hambre
como los perros aquellos con los que tanto he soñado.
Lo acerqué a mi seno duro y el niño empezó a mamar.
Mamaba como un león medio muerto medio vivo.
Mamó hasta que se durmió de nuevo dentro de mí.
¿Cómo se llama mi nieto? y luego me desperté.

How to tell my grandfather that the boy was born in Miami
and will live in Miami and grow up in Miami
and won't speak Spanish, but Spanglish, a language
of barbarians, champions, and emigrant families?
How to tell my grandfather that I've become an emigrant?
Then my grandfather said: bring me your son, you little imp.
And I brought him my son wrapped in my own shirt,
naked, asleep, and in the dream the wind blew.
My grandfather held the kid by the feet, swinging him around,
and I screamed in horror, I was going to die of fright.
If he survives, he's my grandson, said my grandfather, dizzy.
The boy opened his eyes a couple times, I'm dying!
The boy was alive and he was as hungry
as all those dogs I've dreamed of so often.
I brought him to my hard breast and the boy began to suck.
He sucked like a lion, half-dead, half-alive.
He sucked until he fell asleep again inside me.
What's my grandson's name? And then I woke up.

INDEX

A

I DON'T BELIEVE IN POETRY| LEGNA RODRÍGUEZ IGLESIAS

Made in Miami Beach ~ Printing as needed

◊◊◊

2024